Robert Houston McCready

The First Presbyterian Church, Chester, N.Y., 1798-1898

Robert Houston McCready

The First Presbyterian Church, Chester, N.Y., 1798-1898

ISBN/EAN: 9783337261085

Printed in Europe, USA, Canada, Australia, Japan

Cover: Foto ©Lupo / pixelio.de

More available books at **www.hansebooks.com**

CHURCH AND PARSONAGE, 1898

THE FIRST

PRESBYTERIAN CHURCH

CHESTER, N. Y.

1798-1898.

ROBERT HOUSTON McCREADY, Pastor.

CHESTER, N. Y.
June, 1898.

1798=1898.

To all who love the Chester Presbyterian Church, members and friends, are these pages most affectionately dedicated.

May the memory of the struggles and successes of this first Hundred years thrill you and inspire you to make the Twentieth Century a sublime monument of Christian activity for the salvation of souls.

A Historical Sketch

....V....

The First Presbyterian Church of Chester, N. Y.

WITH ITS MINISTERS AND ELDERS: ALSO THE THREE DEACONS AND SEVERAL TRUSTEES SERVING THE CHURCH DURING THE MINISTRY OF THE PRESENT PASTOR.

IT WAS PREPARED SPECIALLY AS A PART OF THE CELEBRATION OF THE CHURCH BUILDING ERECTED IN CHESTER IN 1798.

NO RECORD OF THE EXACT DATE OF DEDICATION BEING LEFT, JUNE 5, 6 AND 7 HAVE BEEN CHOSEN AS THE MOST FITTING SEASON OF THE YEAR. IT IS THE MONTH OF ROSES AND GROWTH OF HIGH HOPES AND SPLENDID ASPIRATIONS.

THIS RECORD OF THE CENTURY MAKES NO CLAIM TO BE COMPLETE, BUT IT IS ACCURATE AND TRUE TO THE FACTS SO FAR AS THEY CAN BE LEARNED.

MAY IT INSPIRE YOU TO WRITE THE FAMILY RECORD VERY PLAIN AND IN SUCH GODLY DEEDS AND WELL SHAPED CHARACTERS AS CAN BE EASILY READ BY HIM WHO FOLLOWS IN WRITING THE NEXT HISTORY.

Pastors.

REV. S. R. JONES,	1798—1805
REV. DANIEL CRANE,	1805—1808
REV. NOAH COE,	1811–1814
REV. JAMES H. THOMAS,	1814—1827
REV. JOHN B. FISH,	1830—1835
REV. ISAAC C. BEACH,	1835—1845
REV. JAMES W. WOOD, D.D.,	1846—1862
REV. THOMAS NICHOLS,	1863—1871
REV. T. A. LEGGETT, D.D.,	1872—1881
REV. THOMAS C. BEATTIE,	1882—1888
REV. JOHN F. BURROWS, D.D.,	1889—1894
REV. ROBERT H. McCREADY, Ph.D.,	1894—

Historical Record

1798=1898

THE erection of the first Church building in any community is a great event. It was especially so in Chester when our present organization built and dedicated its first local habitation in 1798. It had been in the minds of the people to erect a house of worship long before the Revolutionary war broke out. They had even hewn and drawn some of the logs when the call to arms forced them to lay down the adz and take up the rifle.

The bugle had sounded a call for the defence of their civil liberty. They answered it as became the men who lived in the land of the Pilgrim fathers. God gave them victory; made their land free and independent, and they came back to finish the work in gratitude which had been so splendidly begun before they went away.

The Church society had taken on various forms and had passed through many trying experiences before its final entrance into the General Assembly Presbyterian Church in 1813. It began in a very humble way. It was the custom of these early settlers to meet for worship in the houses of the different families. When the little log school-house was erected it became the centre of interest and all meetings, religious and political, were held there. There were, no doubt, some among these earliest settlers about Chester who held their membership in the Churches at Blooming Grove, Goshen, and other points. Rev. Simeon R. Jones, leaves this on record when he settled in Chester as the first pastor in 1799. "I found five females in Chester who were members of adjoining Churches and one praying man, William Vail." We are curious, therefore, to find out all we can as to the character of these early settlers since such a few of them have developed a very tenacious purpose to build a Church.

As early as 1704 we find one, Daniel Cromline, purchasing an interest in the Wawayanda patent. He was a merchant in the vicinity of New York, but was anxious to open up the territory he had secured in the vicinity of Grey Court and Chester. In 1716 he secured the services of a young English mason, William Bull, to build what is known as the "Old Greycourt House" on the road between Chester and Craigville. The increase of settlers was not very rapid, but we find a few families still living here like the Bulls, Durlands, Carpenters, Drakes, Roes, Seelys, Yelvertons, Holberts and Jacksons, who trace the settlement of their ancestors in Chester and vicinity to many years before the Revolutionary War.

Mr. Alfred Roe, an elder in the Church, and a sketch of whom is found in this volume, and who represents a large relationship in this vicinity has definite knowledge that his great grandfather purchased their present farm in 1751. Charles R. Bull, a most genial, helpful Churchman of the Presbyterians, represents a large relationship descended from William Bull. It is conceded, also, that John Yelverton settled in the village of Chester and laid out the plot for the town as early as 1751, and that the Durland family was on the ground as early as 1756.

English blood was evidently the first on the field, or predominated sufficiently later to give the name Chester to the town. Thus we find English, Welch and Scotch blood as the foundation of the settlement of Chester, and the elements which struggled through nearly half a century of adversity before they could plant a house of worship in their midst.

In 1783, or immediately after the war with Great Britain, Abijah Yelverton made an effort to concentrate the religious forces of the town on erecting a Church. He led the movement by offering to donate an acre of land where the Wash-

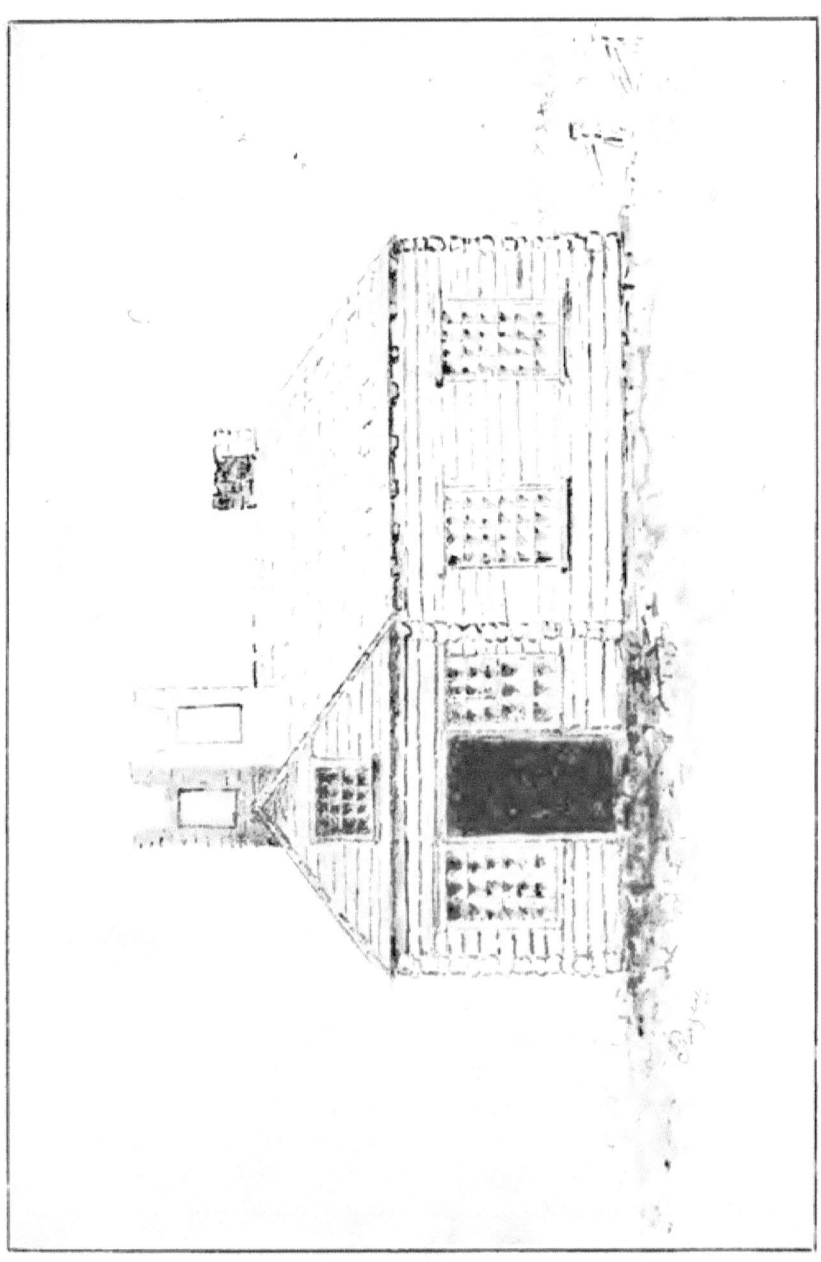

THIS LOG CHURCH WAS DEDICATED IN 1758.

ington Hotel now stands. Mr. Yelverton's name does not appear upon the Church roll. His wife, however, was a very earnest Christian woman, and many members of the family were adherents of the Church. This may account for Mr. Yelverton's deep interest in the Church and the religious wellfare of the town.

The war had so weakened their forces, which before it broke out consisted only of about thirty families, that they felt unequal to the task of building a Church. The Rev. Silas Constant's appearing among them about this time greatly encouraged and inspired them. He urged their immediate acceptance of Mr. Yelverton's offer, and the site for the Church was secured.

But it was not until fourteen years later, or in 1797, that they were able to begin the construction of the Church. At the close of the year they had erected a log Church at a cost of $1,509.28. It was by no means a finished building. It was enclosed and made fit for service, however, in 1798. The exact day of the opening can not now be determined, but it was a day of great joy and rejoicing among the people of Chester. The congregation continued between those rough, unfinished walls for three years, praising God for His goodness, thankful if they could get their toes anywhere near the little foot-stove of the fortunate few. Temporary seats of rough hewn logs or boards, were used by the hearers as they listened to the long sermon, while a rude oak platform and pulpit of the same material served the preacher for all occasions.

This Church of a Sabbath morning presented quite a contrast to the well-furnished churches of the present day. These have their richly cushioned seats, with downy back rests, arranged on the plan of the famous amphitheatre; pulpits, elevated, spacious, and finished with beautifully upholstered furniture; handsomely carpeted floors; stained or opalescent glass windows inwrought with the most poetical and beautiful figures which the genius of art can design; powerful and melodious organs pouring forth the faintest, sweetest tones or filling the worshipper with awe as the whole house quivers under its tones of bass, while every wall and nook and corner is filled by painters' art or tapestry, and the entire Church is filled with the balmy air of the tropics and lighted in an instant with the brilliancy of the sun.

Yet the worship offered to God at that time was likely as sincere and as acceptable to Him as that offered to Him now in the midst of all these splendors.

The congregation was not yet organized as a church when it invited its first regular minister, Rev. Samson R. Jones, to labor among them at a salary of $75.00 per annum.

He was also to have the privilege of teaching the village school to piece out his support.

Rev. S. R. Jones began his labors in Chester in the Spring of 1798, and proved himself most efficient.

The Church grew in numbers and wealth, and in the course of four years the building was comfortably finished and furnished at a cost of $1,692.40, making the total cost of the Church $3,082.68. The log seats had given place to square pews, the fashion of the day.

A round box pulpit was introduced, and the house of worship became so crowded that galleries were erected on three sides of the Church, while the steeple set off the outside with the air of a real temple of worship.

It made no pretensions of being a model of artistic taste and beauty either externally or internally. Yet its purpose was well known to every passer-by.

The deep interest in the Church and her future was manifested by the amount they paid for pews. The amount aggregated about $2,000, which for those times was a very large sum. This enabled the congregation to dedicate the Church free of debt and leave a balance in the treasury.

The Church, which had been so long in construction and final equipment, was at length formally dedicated on Sept. 19th, 1802.

Rev. Mr. Jones was still its successful Pastor. His

salary had been sufficiently increased to enable him to live. He had also been relieved from the added burden of teaching.

Mr. Jones has left on record a small pen picture of the people in his time:

"Their prevailing amusements (I need not say very fashionable vices) were card playing, attending balls, horse racing and not always temperate drinking. Generally their attendance on public worship on Sabbath, though good from first to last, might be considered among their pleasing amusements. They were friendly, sociable, liberal and often generous to their minister, feasting him at his own and their tables on roast turkey, etc. One very unnatural custom was prevalent at Chester—the custom of drinking wine and spirits at funerals. This custom I successfully opposed. With the fashionable vices the people mixed religious instruction. I took great pains to instruct them in the doctrines of the Gospel and their covenant obligations. They were zealous and prayerful."

It is said that when they were received into Presbytery that body was very pleasantly disappointed with their satisfactory examination.

On August 30th, 1803, the congregation, which had grown very considerably, was organized into a church under the care of the Morris County and West Chester Associate Presbytery.

The charter members were only twenty-one in number, but this gives no idea of the strength of the congregation, as will be readily seen from the sale of the pews, which amounted to $2,000 the year before.

Of the twenty-one original charter members six were men and fifteen were women. Their names ought not to be forgotten. The following is the list, lacking but one name which can not be found: MALES.

Seth Marvin, James Foster,
Jonathan Hallock, William Vail,
Samuel Harlow, Jesse Cooly.

FEMALES.

Rosanna Kinner,
Elizabeth Hallock, wife
  of Jonathan.
Ruth Vail,
Julia Holly,
Mary Mapes,
Ann Cooley,
Sarah Little,

Bertha Kinner,
Hannah Hallock,
Eliza Satterly,
Sarah Marvin,
Susanna Holbert,
Eunice Popino,
Lavinna Feagles.

These, with many others of different nationalities and whose names do not appear in this list, were God-fearing church men, who prized their Christian privileges, laboring earnestly and faithfully to enlarge the kingdom of the Master.

General Seth Marvin and Jonathan Hallock were the first deacons of the congregation. The first communion was celebrated on Oct. 2nd, 1803. The Church was packed to its utmost and many could not obtain an entrance.

In the following year, 1804, there were many members added to the Church, bringing the number up to sixty-two.

The ministry of Mr. Jones, which closed in 1805, was prosperous from the very beginning. He was young and full of earnest zeal for the cause of Christ while he labored at Chester. His departure after six years of toil, was much lamented. He was born in Essex Co., N. J., in 1773, and died at the ripe age of 84 years.

In the Spring of 1805, and shortly after the close of Mr. Jones' ministry, the Rev. Daniel Crane was called to be his successor. He served the Church for three years most acceptably, but severed his relations with it because of difficulties growing out of its organization. He left, however, with the good will of the congregation, for he was recalled in 1827, and served the Church again for three years.

He was no doubt influential in having the Chester Church apply, not to its own Presbytery, but to the Hudson Presbytery of the General Assembly Presbyterian Church in the United States of America, for supplies.

In April, 1809, the trustees of the congregation did make such an application. Owing to the dissolution, about this time, of the Presbytery under which they had been organized they may also have expressed a desire to be taken under the care of Hudson Presbytery.

In 1810 the Chester Church was taken under the care of the Hudson Presbytery, and thus became a child of the General Assembly Presbyterian Church in the U. S. of America. She still retained so many of her independent privileges that the Presbytery was not certain of her status until three years later, when on April 8th, 1813, the Church and congregation, by a public vote, adopted the Presbyterian form of Church government and became a thoroughly Presbyterian congregation.

A few days later, and under the direction of the Presbytery, an election for elders was held, which resulted in the choice of the two deacons, General Seth Marvin and Jonathan Hallock with William Vail and William Gray.

Mr. Gray declined to serve, but the others were solemnly ordained to their office on the following Sabbath, April 18th, 1813. In September of that same year two more elders, Elnathan Satterly and Abraham Stickney, were added to the Session. The Church had been some time without a regular Pastor; but on April 12th, 1811, the Church called Mr. Noah Coe as the successor of Rev. Daniel Crane.

Mr. Noah Coe was ordained and installed as Pastor, July 3rd, 1811, the Presbytery meeting in Chester at that time. Rev. Noah Coe's pastorate was very brief, ending in the following Spring of 1814. On August 23rd of the same year a unanimous call was then extended to James H. Thomas, who was ordained and installed Pastor October 12th of the same year. Mr. Thomas was engaged, however, for only two-thirds of his time. The Rev. Dr. Frieland, formerly pastor of Monroe, thinks the other third of his time was given to that place. His salary from the Chester Church is stated by Dr. Leggett to have been $333.34.

A severe loss was sustained by the Church in the death, within a year, of her two oldest officers, General Seth Marvin, who died Aug. 25th, 1815, and Jonathan Hallock, who passed away on March 16th, 1816. They had borne a conspicuous part in all the changes through which the Church had passed.

The necessity for an increased number of active officers had been strongly felt for some time. A meeting was called for this purpose, to be held March 23rd, 1816, which resulted in the election of Joseph Sherwood and Ebenezer Holbert. This was only one week after the death of Mr. Hallock. Thus quickly does the Church recuperate her forces and equip herself for the work entrusted to her by Christ.

The church seemed to be in a good working condition about this time. But it required four years more of untiring labor and faithful preaching before the visible working of the Spirit was manifest in the hearts of the people.

In the meantime, however, the people were showing their good will toward the Church, and the servants of the Lord who ministered to them in divine things, by making an effort to purchase a parsonage.

On September 16th, 1818, a subscription paper was passed through the congregation with this object in view. On it we find a few names for liberal sums, such as follows:

Elnathan Satterly,	$60.00	James Murray Muller,	$110.00
Joseph Sherwood,	50.00	Cash,	20.00
Michael Denton,	50.00	Townsend Seely,	15.00
Ebenezer Holbert,	40.00	James Holbert,	25.00
John Holbert,	40.00		

This money is to be paid to the following Board of Trustees, under very guarded restrictions as to its use:

Elnathan Satterly,   Samuel Durland,
Henry Seely,   Michael Denton,
John Springstead,   Samuel Pitts,
Cornelius Board,   Abraham Stickney.

Rev. Mr. Thomas had been very untiring in his efforts to build up the Church, and his labor was not in vain. In the

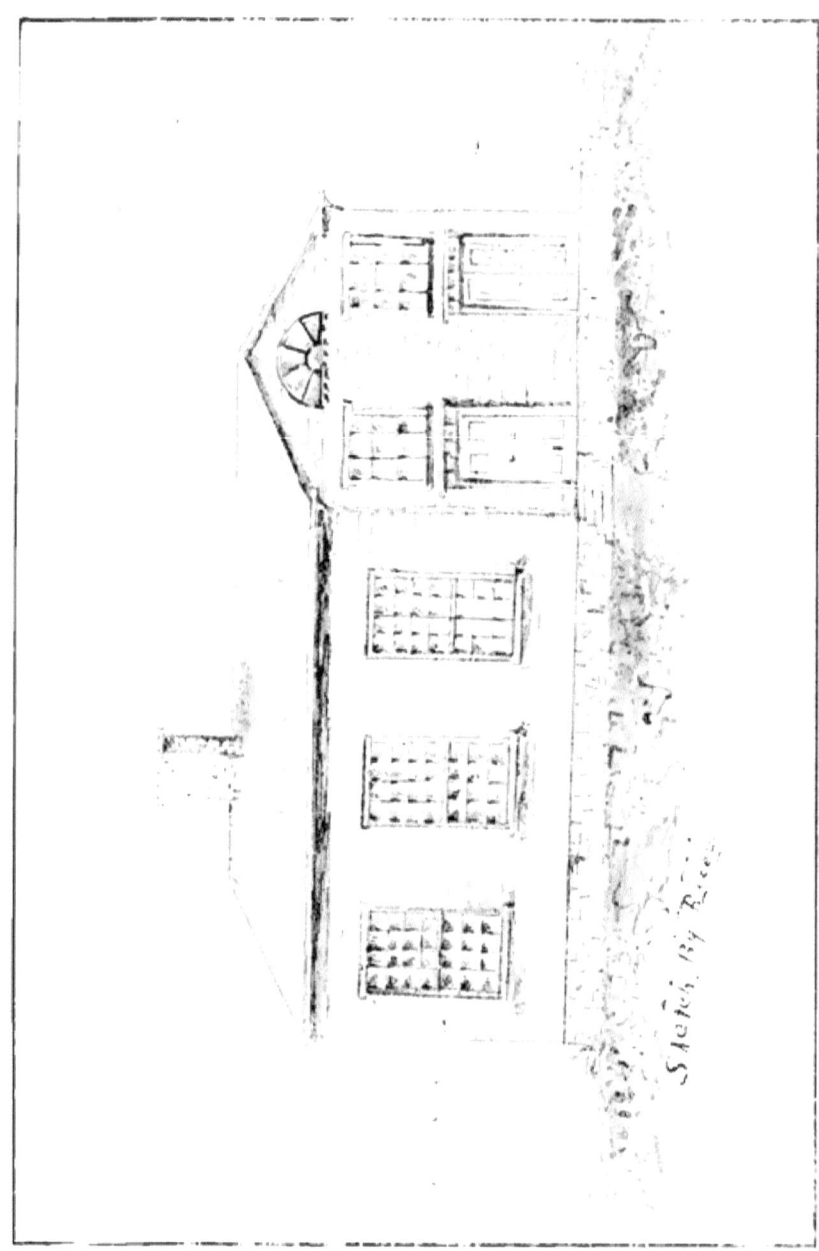

Sketch by Rice.

Drafted by GEORGE BASKER.

THIS CHURCH WAS DEDICATED IN 1829.

Winter of 1820 and '21 there were 140 souls added to the Church. With these additions the Church now numbered 204 members. Two new members were also added to the Session—James Holbert and Townsend Seely. Mr. Thomas was recognized in his own day and for half a century after his ministry in Chester ceased "as an affectionate spiritual Pastor, a wise counsellor, and a faithful friend."

After thirteen years of faithful service his pastorate ceased on April 18, 1827. It may have been that he felt unable to move the people to secure a new Church edifice, and felt that the Church had reached the summit of its prosperity until a new edifice should be built.

The Rev. Daniel Crane—who had been the Pastor for three years, from 1805 to 1808—being open to a call, was, on July 9th, 1827, recalled, and later installed by the Presbytery. His second pastorate of three years is noteworthy for two things. He persuaded the congregation to build a new Church on a new site, while he pushed on Church trial after Church trial in disciplining the people, as had his predecessor, and according to the custom of the times.

This second Church was built on the site of the present Cemetery. The reason for this change of location was based on the expectation that the village would grow in that direction. The location was evidently from the beginning as unsatisfactory as the Church building. It was a low, narrow, long, bare edifice. It had no shape, no spire, no gallery except a small loft for the Choir placed over the pulpit. The pulpit was located, according to the custom of the day, between the two doors at the front. The surroundings and the Church were most uninviting when it was dedicated in 1829. Whether the uncouthness of the building or the dissatisfaction among the people had anything to do with the health of Rev. Mr. Crane is not now known, but he was compelled to resign in 1830 on account of failing health.

The Church remained without a Pastor for more than eighteen months. At the end of that time Rev. John B. Fish, spoken of as a man "of great meekness, full of faith and the Holy Ghost," seems to have acted as Pastor of the Chester Church for three years.

There having been no call regularly presented through the Presbytery, and objections having been raised as to his continuing to serve this Church while he belonged to North River Presbytery, his labors were discontinued.

The Rev. Isaac C. Beach was the next minister called. His pastorate continued for ten years, and was signally crowned by God's deepening the spiritual life and gathering many into the Church, especially in the years 1836 and 1837, and later in the Winter of 1841.

Twenty additional pews were added to the Church, which, under the inspiring preaching and helpful ministry of Mr. Beach, was filled to overflowing. In 1835 three new Elders were added to the congregation, they were Philo Greggory, Nathaniel Rocket, and John H. Tuthill. The Church took on a new spirit and the work of the Lord made steady and marked progress.

Elnathan Satterly, who had served as Elder since the entrance of the Church into the General Assembly died October 19th, 1836. He was followed to the Church triumphant by Elder Joseph Sherwood, who died in December, 1838. Mr. Jesse Roe and Mr. Ira H. Hawkins, men who are still well known to this generation, were chosen to fill the vacant places.

Besides the assistance rendered by several brother ministers, Mr. Beach was ably assisted by Timothy Lester. Mr. Lester was a young man who had been thoroughly converted, and was so devoted to Christ in making known his salvation to others that he made a deep impression upon many young men wherever he spoke. Our oldest Elder, Mr. Gabriel Seely, a man who has been the instrument in God's hand of doing much good, dates his conversion to the time of Mr. Lester's first labors in Chester. His memory is still cherished by some of the older people, and he was greatly beloved throughout this whole region, where he assisted many of the brethren in their revival work. But he was not allowed to continue his labors long on the earth. In 1842 he made his home with Elder Jesse Roe, where he was ill for a little while when the Master called him to the joy of his rich reward. Surely he realized in the very fullest sense the blessing of the promise, "They that be wise shall shine as the brightness of the firmament, and they that turn many to righteousness as the stars forever and ever."

Mr. Beach, whose work had proved so eminently successful, closed his labors in Chester in 1845, and was dismissed to labor in the bounds of the North River Presbytery.

In the same year—November 1st—the Rev. James Washington Wood, D.D., brother of Daniel T. Wood, the beloved Pastor for twenty-nine years of First Middletown Congregation, was called to Chester. He was installed Pastor on January 27th, 1846.

Sketch of Some of the Ministers.

The history of the Church is so interwoven with the ministers who serve her, that it has been thought well to weave the two together under the above title.

Very little can be said of the ministers previous to this time, since little or no record of their life is to be found anywhere.

Rev. James W. Wood, D.D.

MR. WOOD was "of the Manor born." He belonged to the once large Wood family in Orange County. By marriage the well-known families, in the county, of the Armstrongs, Wisners, Vails, Dusenburys, McDowells, Seelys, Dunnings, Woods, were united, and a friendly intercourse existed which gave an abundance of wholesome pleasure to social life. The house of Mr. Wood's birth stands on the west side of the road between Florida and Warwick, about one-half a mile from the first-named town.

The immigrating ancestor of the family was Timothy Wood (1) from Yorkshire, England. Timothy landed in this country in 1700, and joined his brother Jonas, then living near Huntington, Long Island. In 1727 Timothy was killed by the Indians. His body was found pierced with seven poisoned arrows. He left three sons, Timothy, Daniel (II) and Andrew. The two older sons moved to Orange County in the Spring of 1728. Timothy settled in Goshen, Daniel (II.) near Florida, and Andrew moved to New England.

Daniel, (II.) the ancestor of this sketch, bought in 1733 what was afterwards called "the Wood farm" for one dollar an acre, and for 112 years it remained in the family. By a first wife there were these children : John, Jonas, Mary, Elizabeth, and Deborah. By a second wife there were two sons, Daniel and Andrew (III.).

Daniel became a physician, and served in the army as a surgeon during the Revolution. His record is most excellent. His son John founded Quincy, Ill., and became Governor of the State.

Andrew (III.) continued at the homestead. He married a cousin, Elizabeth Wood, daughter of John Wood, from Longford, Ireland, thus uniting two branches which had separated in the old country. The children by this marriage were Jesse Wood, Elizabeth Totten, Andrew Wood (who became a Methodist minister in Ohio), and James Wood (IV).

James Wood (IV.) was born April 18th, 1778. He remained at the homestead, and in addition to farming learned the trade of a cabinet maker and carpenter. A high clock frame, made by him as a wedding gift to his bride, and now (1897) owned by a descendant in Easton, Pa., illustrates his handiwork. He married March 9, 1799, Mary Armstrong. This Francis Armstrong sailed from Ulster County, Ireland, August 6th, 1728, and landed in New York, December 10th, 1728. He was a straight, strict and trusted Presbyterian. He was one of the founders of the Presbyterian Church at Florida, and his character may be pictured from the following "memorandum," copied from the original, as written by Rev. J. Elmer, Pastor, September 11th, 1758 :

"Mr. Francis Armstrong, Elder of the Presbyterian Congregation in Florida, has in every article fulfilled his obligation to me as a Minister on the account of my support while I lived in the congregation, and much more than ever was his proportion for which I do forever acquit him from all subscription made to me, and heartily and earnestly recommend him as an example to others which if they would follow they need not want a preached gospel." J. ELMER.

"September 11th, 1758."

A mixture with the Armstrongs added to those essentials needed in strong, good men.

James Wood (IV.) purchased of the family the farm, paying $25.00 per acre for which his great-grandfather paid $1.00 per acre. From the marriage of James Wood and Mary Armstrong were born Daniel T., Sarah, William, Julia, Caroline, Jane, Keturah, James (IV.), Mary, Thomas and Emily. Daniel T. was for twenty-nine years Pastor of the Presbyterian Church in Middletown. William was an Elder in the Presbyterian Church, Galesburg, Ill. Jane was for many years engaged in missionary and pastoral work as an assistant to Rev. Thos. K. Beecher, Elmira, N. Y.

James Washington Wood (IV.), or "Dominie Wood," as he was called by the seniors in Chester, was born near Florida, Monday, October 5th, 1813. He remained at home until nearly nineteen years of age. At a revival service in Florida during the Fall of 1831 he became interested in Christ by repentance and faith. He made a public profession January 1st, 1832, by uniting with the Presbyterian Church in Florida. His mind naturally turned to a calling in life, and with the knowledge that an education was costly, and means did not exist to aid him, he nevertheless determined to prepare for the ministry.

In the Spring of 1832 he began a course of studies with his brother, Rev. Daniel T. Wood, in Middletown. The sudden change from an active outdoor life to the sedentary habits of the student brought on a severe sickness, so it was necessary to carry him on a bed to his Florida home. In the Fall of 1832 he entered the Goshen Academy, then under the charge of a Mr. Stark. In November, 1833, he went by the once famous Newburg & Easton stage line to Easton, Pa., and on December 11th, 1833. was admitted as a student in Lafayette College. In this institution he held a high rank, and sustained himself by working as a cabinet maker, or carpenter, by teaching and by writing for newspapers and magazines. He graduated September 20th, 1837, and in honor for his records as a student and orator was awarded the Latin and English Salutatory Address on Commencement Day. Next he entered the Union Theological Seminary in New York City, and accepted such occupations as would bring in funds for support. For three months, one year, he established a class in the classics in Middletown. This effort in the plane of a higher education resulted in the establishment of the Academy in that city. During a meeting of the Presbytery of Hudson, at Amity, Orange County, N. Y., on September 11th, 1839, Mr. Wood was examined and licensed by the Presbytery to the office of Minister. His hours while a student at Lafayette had not been given exclusively to study. The attractions of society had their share, which resulted in an engagement between Elizabeth Caroline Able and James Washington Wood. They were married October 9th, 1839, in Easton, by Rev. Daniel T. Wood, of Middletown, N. Y. and Rev. Dr. Gray, of Easton, Pa.

Mrs. Wood was the daughter of Jacob Able, the son of Jacob Able, who, when a child, came from Germany in the year 1750. The Able house at " he point " still stands where the several generations of the family lived. They were Presbyterians, industrious, frugal, and prosperous. Mrs. Wood was well educated, a persistent reader, and possessed a remarkable memory. In early life she was active in Easton society, and earnest in the work of a Sabbath School scholar and teacher. At the age of eighteen she united with the Presbyterian Church in Easton, under the pastorship of Rev. Dr. Gray. Through her life, as a Pastor's wife, she appreciated and supported all objects of benevolence, yet preferred the home duties of a wife and mother than to be the president of a sewing circle. In the congregation where her husband was Pastor she was popular, and equally maintained her part as "the better half." Mrs. Wood died at her home in Allentown, Pa., April 6, 1882.

The children of this marriage were Jacob Winslow Wood, Allentown, Pa.; James Whitfield Wood, Easton, Pa.;

Elizabeth Able Harrison, Minneapolis, Minn.; and Daniel Burton Wood, Spokane, Mo. Subsequently Mr. Wood formed a second marriage with Miss Maria Woodring of Allentown, Pa.

Mr. Wood was ordained and installed as Pastor of the Presbyterian Church in Deckertown, N. J., December 11th, 1839, by the Presbytery of Rockaway. A handsome memorial window in the new Presbyterian Church in Deckertown is a witness of the esteem with which Mr. Wood is remembered by the sons and daughters of his old parishioners in that place In September, 1845, he resigned, and began work for the American Board Foreign Missions in New York. As the representative of this society he preached for missions in Chester, N. Y., and unexpectedly to him the congregation extended a call for him to become their Pastor. This invitation was accepted, and he began his work in Chester, November 1st, 1845. He remained in Chester seventeen years, during which time the Church more than doubled in members and in reality valuation. About 216 members were added, and a large and beautiful new house of worship was erected in 1853 on a more desirable site at a cost of about $10.000. Feeling the need of relaxation, Mr. Wood resigned October 1st, 1862, and moved to Easton, Pa. On October 18th, 1862, he sailed from New York for a visit to Europe and the Holy Land, returning in the Fall of 1863. On April 23d, 1865, he accepted a call to the Presbyterian Church in the City of Allentown, Pa., and was installed by the Presbytery of Philadelphia, October 25th, 1865. He continued to reside in Allentown until his death, which occurred suddenly May 5th, 1884, at one o'clock, a. m.

Mr. and Mrs. Wood are buried in the Able family plot in the beautiful cemetery at Easton, Pa.

Mr. Wood was of medium size, brown hair, blue eyes, good form, and was regarded an attractive man in his appearance. During his life he was a hard student, continuing his acquaintance with the classics, and in the German and French languages, as well as the writings in the English tongue. He was well equipped as an educator and preacher. On July 2d, 1879, the degree of "Doctor Divinitatis" was conferred on him by his Alma Mater, Lafayette College, to which he responded in an oration in the Latin tongue. He was a frequent contributor to the newspapers and general publications, both secular and of the church, and was frequently called upon for prepared addresses on popular occasions. Throughout life he was young in his feelings and sympathies. No greater enjoyment could be given him than to be in the company of the young people. The sports of youth were pleasures to him, and at heart he continued young. As an associate he was a brilliant conversationalist, and could adapt himself to the acts and thoughts of those around him, making every one feel easy and friendly. The old and the young, the poor and the distressed, looked to him as a champion without the fear of disappointment. His life in society and in the church was a brilliant harvest.

His voice was clear, his oratory fair, his manner in the pulpit enthusiastic, and it was common for him to clinch a point with a stamp of the foot or with a blow on the desk. Sometimes he would write and read his sermons from manuscript, sometimes extemporize, and sometimes commit to memory. He was available as a talker, and was usually prepared for a speech by reason of an extensive equipment gathered from continuous readings and studying the events of the day and signs of the times. He wrote a plain hand, and was accurate in the composition. To him the English language was rich in words for expressing thought, and therefore seldom mixed words or phrases of a strange tongue with his sentences. The Anglo-Saxon was his model in text.

To his calling as a Minister he devoted every talent, and his love for the work warmed him to daily efforts in the cause. He was open, he was frank, honest and determined. With his mind once convinced and his duty clear to himself, no man or emergency could swerve him from his work. He opposed the wrong as it appeared to him, and advocated the right under every circumstance. As a Preacher and Pastor he held it his duty to fight sin and errors, whether in the Church or out of the Church. He regarded the life of man as a whole and one compact effort. To him it was wrong for a man to sin on Monday and pray on Sunday. By his life, by his writings, by his preaching he opposed such. He held that Christianity covered all things, and ought to influence mankind in every phase of life. By his interpretation the teachings of Christ taught men how to work, how to play, as well as how to pray. He saw the right side in religion, in politics, in society, and he championed his views with his whole power, and with an earnestness and honesty which won the respect and hearts of his opponents. No one could fail to learn his opinion on any topic if they sought it, and his counsel and advice were always filled with an affection and earnestness which attracted the hearer. He loved those whom he served, and never forgot or neglected a friend. His attachments were bound in his heart with chains of steel. Though dead, he is not forgotten.

Mr. Wood was one of the early abolitionists in the country. He thought slavery a sin and an institution injurious to the country, and a gross wrong towards the black men. In earlier days there were slaves in the Wood family. When liberated the unfortunate Africans were provided for during life. It may be the positive ideas of justice and equality were instilled in his mind through home influences and teachings. One fact connected with his youth has been thought a factor in moulding his life and governing his actions on the slavery question. The Sewards in Florida were neighbors. The children of the two families were inseparable. One of their associates was James Bertolf, a colored boy. The intimacies continued through life. Maybe the colored boy Bertolf made such an impression as to lead his associates in the advanced ranks of the Abolitionists. Perhaps the recollections of Bertolf incited the thought which led Senator

Seward to declare his allegiance to that "Higher Law," as compared with any statutes which enslaved men, and the same power may have influenced Mr. Wood to undertake an active interest in the "Underground Railway" filled with all of its hazardous risks. The parsonage became the "depot," and many fugitive slaves, traveling under the guidance of "The Underground Railway," were secreted in and about Mr. Wood's home. The agents were enthusiastic and determined in the work. A large business was done and it seemed ample funds were always ready for any emergency. The adjoining agencies were located near Pompton, N. J., in Florida, and in Elmira. From thence, to Canada. Mr. Wood regarded his record on the slavery question, and his connection with "The Ungerground Railway" as one of the most satisfactory features of his life.

Subsequently Mr. Wood said of the people, "Through every trial He has brought this flock in safety. "He has trained this Church as one of its vines. "He has always moved some to be deeply interested in the Zion of this place, whose money, time and influence have often been freely rendered. Let us tell our children then of God's mercies and kindness in times past, and receive ourselves fresh inducements to devotedness in the service of our God."

The young men and women into whose hands the Chester Church is now held have no struggle with poverty or frontier life. A brighter and stronger generation surround them The influences of a more advanced life call for quicker and better acts. The gage is higher, and the goal harder to reach. May the children now in command in the Church meet every expectation, in the richest fullness thereof, and may they realize those "mercies and kindness" which have been measured to their parents.

It was during Dr. Woods' time that the Church made the most marked progress of her history. There is no doubt that the interest which he awakened in the building of a new Church added greatly to the devotion of the people in building up the Spiritual Kingdom of Christ. This was a great year for erecting Churches. The society of Presbyterians at Monroe, felt the need of a new building and erected their present building.

The Methodist Church of Chester was also built about this year. They had been holding meetings in Chester in various places ever since 1837. Chester was ministered to by the M. E. preacher at Sugar Loaf. At length they thought themselves strong enough to have a Church of their own. It was a great work for them, but it was nobly executed. They have now the finest gem of a frame M. E. Church in the county. It is finished with cathedral glass and beautiful decorations.

The Presbyterians were stirred up by all this spirit of Church building about them to build something more suitable to the times. After a most careful examination by the minister and officers of the Church the present excellent site was chosen for the new Church building. Their reasoning is quite evident to-day.

The Erie Railroad had come within half a mile of the old village of Chester. It was very desirable that the Church should keep pace with the changes of the community, both as to location and in the structure of the building. Accordingly the present large and handsome structure for those times was completed, at at cost, says Mr. Wood, of $10,000, and dedicated January 4th, 1854.

This was the third Church edifice erected by this organization, and while it has taken on some improvements since that time it remains substantially the same as when first built. A beautiful Sunday School and lecture room has been added to the rear. This was done during the pastorate of Rev. T. C. Beattie, now of the First Church, Albequerque, New Mexico. Even the bell found its place in the tower when the Church was first erected, having been donated by Thomas Powell, of Newburgh, the friend of many Churches and as a special favor to Mrs. Elizabeth Seely and Mrs. Dr. J. W. Wood, the Pastor's wife. The seating capacity of the Church was originally about 600. It has been modified, however, by the introduction of a large pipe organ during the pastorate of the late Rev. John Burrows, D.D.

Rev. Thos. Nichols.

ONLY one month passed after the formal resignation of Dr. Wood, when the Church secured the permanent services of the young and handsome theological student, Thomas Nichols.

He was just fresh from the seminary. He was, it is thought, one of the best equipped men that has ever preached in Chester. He had been sitting at the feet of such theologians as Prof. H. B. Smith, of Union, and later of Prof. W. S. T. Shedd, then of Andover, but later filling the chair with princely acceptance at Union. He represented the new school side of the Church and was full of zeal in the feeding of the people with truly gospel food. He was tested very severely as a young man for five months during the Winter of 1862 and '63, and then on March 11, 1863, the people stood up and said "this is the man we want for our under shepherd in Christ. We shall support him with our money and love as long as the Lord shall keep him among us doing such work as this."

He was ordained and installed on March 11th, 1863. Rev. Joseph McNulty, D.D., of Montgomery, preaching the sermon. A little more than a month later he brought among his people Anna M. Boyd, of Owego, a blushing bride, who was henceforth to be the sharer of all his toils and sorrows and joys. From the day of their marriage, April, 22d, 1863, she has been doing her part as a faithful ministers wife, beloved by all who know her. All the Chester girls wondered how he should have found a wife in Owego. They knew he had been born in Yonkers, N. Y., the date, February 5th, 1838, is added now as possibly a new item of interest. The secret of it, however, lay in the fact that he went to Owego Academy, Owego, N. Y., to prepare for College. He passed from this preparatory school to the College of New Jersey (Princeton), from which he graduated in 1856. It was not until two years after graduating that he began a Christian life and decided to give himself up to the preaching of the Gospel. He entered the Union Seminary in 1858, remaining two years and graduated from Andover Seminary in 1861. He found both his work and his home very congenial to him. His son, Rev. Thomas McBride Nichols, the eldest of his five children, and Pastor of the Market Square Presbyterian Church, Philadelphia, Pa., was born here.

To the more than two hundred members which Mr. Nichols found on the Church roll when he came, were added one hundred members lacking one during his pastorate. He also made seventy-eight lives happy at the marriage altar, and comforted the friends of a hundred and twelve souls who passed from life into death.

The deep appreciation of the people was manifest by the addition of $200 more to his salary at the close of his second year, and the continuation of it during all the years that he remained. The excitement of the Civil War was at its height about the time he began his ministry in 1863, and yet there is no record of unpleasantness. It speaks well for both people and preacher. He leaves this testimony: "I preached my first sermon in support of the Government the Sabbath after the battle of Gettysburgh. It was not my last, and I had the support of a loyal and patriotic congregation." There were other difficulties also growing out of the times when Mr. Nichols began his ministry in Chester.

The place was suffering considerably from the recent opening of the Lehigh Valley Railroad to Warwick, N. Y. This made Warwick a new business centre and rival. Growth was slower than usual though it has never been rapid. "Changes of property were few, and there was but little building except big barns by the farmers." Yet the place felt a little of the impetus of the national prosperity in the high price paid for milk and for onions. The difficulties of Mr. Nichols' troublous times were greatly smoothed by the strong level-headed, spiritual men that he had associated with him in the Eldership. Where one was weak another was strong, and they held up the hands of the young minister while the battle with evil went forward.

They were James Holbert, Walter H. Conklin, Ira Hawkins, Jesse Roe, George Conklin, Nathaniel Roe, Gabriel Seely, Robert W. Colfax and Jeheil I. Clark. Just before Mr. Nichols passed to his new field of labor, having preached his farewell sermon June 4th, 1871, Mr. Ira Hawkins fell asleep in Christ, very much lamented by all, and especially by his Pastor. Mr. Nichols, who has still many warm friends in Chester, is now pleasantly located at Milford, Pa., which is within the bounds of the same Presbytery that ordained him.

Rev. Theodore A. Leggett, D.D.

REV. T. A. Leggett was called to succeed Mr. Nichols. He was the son of Rev. John H. Leggett, and was born at Hopewell, Orange Co., Dec. 20th, 1845. At the age of sixteen he made a public profession of faith, uniting with the Church under his father's ministration in 1861, at Middletown, N. Y. He entered Princeton College in September of the same year, graduating from that eminently Presbyterian institution in June, 1865. So well satisfied was he with Princeton, that he continued there for three years longer, or until 1868, studying theology with such eminent men as the seminary at Princeton boasted at that time.

He was licensed to preach the everlasting Gospel of Christ in April, 1867, one year before he completed his theological course. He was evidently ordained without a charge, but labored faithfully in the vineyard of the Master, at the beautiful Summer resort of Cape May, N. J., for two years.

In 1870 he received a call to become Pastor of the Harlem Presbyterian Church, whither he went, but remained only for a short time. The surroundings of that Church were not at that time either beautiful or hopeful. There was nothing attractive about Harlem for a young man who had been reared among the hills and pleasant people of Orange Co.

While spending a few days' vacation in the vicinity of his boyhood home, he was invited to preach in Chester. He did so. The people learned that he was not averse to a change and so called him to be their Pastor late in the Fall of 1871. He preached quite acceptably to the people during all the Winter months, and was installed Pastor of the First Presbyterian Church of Chester on May 2nd, 1872. He came in just the proper time to reap a large harvest of ingathering. The war issues had been settled. Old scores had been forgotten. The Church had been left in a good working condition by Mr. Nichols. He had sown the seed faithfully. The people were ready for an onward movement. The years 1874 and 1876 and 1880 were specially marked by large additions. There were added during his ministry of ten years about 182 souls to the membership of the Church.

These were among the most prosperous years which the farmers of Chester have ever experienced, and they took pride in repairing and improving both the Church and the parsonage.

Even the salary, it is noted, was increased, as was the case when Mr. Nichols was Pastor, but with a stronger likelihood of remaining at the higher figure. The Country Sociable as a means of raising money seems to have been in the height of its glory at this time. If the contribution on such an occasion fell much below one hundred dollars, the sociable was not looked upon as a success financially.

Dr. Leggett having received a call to West New Brighton Calvary Presbyterian Church, Staten Island, in 1881, felt constrained to accept it. And while he does not forget his Chester parish, and is still jealous of all its interests, he has proved himself a worthy and successful servant of the Lord in West New Brighton. In 1897 the University of New York honored him with the degree of D.D. while his heart was still very heavy, because during that Spring the Lord had removed three of his beloved children to the mansions above.

Rev. Thomas Cumming Beattie.

THE Rev. T. C. Beattie, successor to Dr. Leggett, was born of a ministerial family, and has eminently sustained the glory of the family name as a preacher of the gospel. He was the son of Rev. David Beattie, the beloved Pastor of Scotchtown Presbyterian Church, Orange Co., N. Y., for forty-two years. He was born in Scotchtown, N. Y. July 23d, 1854, with a strong physical constitution which was splendidly developed in his boyhood romps over the rugged hills of Scotchtown. After absorbing what was to be had in the way of education at his own village school, he was sent to the Middletown, N. Y., Academy, where George A. Decker, Esq., now a lawyer of wide repute in Middletown, was then the prominent teacher. At twenty years of age and with a bright career before him, he entered Princeton College.

Very shortly after entering College, however, he was smitten with typhoid fever. It was a very malignant case, and left him after a severe struggle for life, with a much weakened constitution.

He graduated, nevertheless, four years later, very near the head of his class of seventy-eight fellow students, delivering the class oration. He was also one of the six appointed to debate on Commencement Day.

He still looks back to those College years with much gratification, for the teachers in his day, Dr. McCosh, in Philosophy, Lyman Atwater, in Logic, Charles A. Young, in Astronomy, and A. Guizot in Physical Geography, were not only eminent men at that time, but have since become world renowned in their various departments.

After graduating in 1878, and while his studies were still fresh in his mind he spent one year in preparing his younger brother, William, for College. The death of this younger and only brother, William, while in his Junior College year at Princeton, made a deep impression upon him.

Mr. Beattie was converted under his father's preaching while yet a young boy of about 14 years of age, and united with the Scotchtown Presbyterian Church. Under the guidance of the Holy Spirit he chose the ministry as a calling. This shows the character of the man for there is no higher vocation on earth, and he was fully convinced that this was his mission in life. His choice of Union Theological Seminary was not made upon its superior teachers, but because he had lived in Princeton four years and believed that a change of surroundings might be beneficial to him. After one year at Union, however, he was strongly convinced that Princeton was the place for him, because there the Word of God was pre-eminently exalted. In Princeton the guesses and theories of the best scholars were subordinated to the inspired Word.

In his course at Union Seminary he received the lectures of such men as Drs. Shedd, Hitchcock, Schaff and Briggs. While at Princeton Seminary his instructors were Drs. A. A. Hodge, Casper Hodge, Aiken, Green and Moffat. He was one of the four speakers appointed for the Commencement exercises of the Seminary. He had been taken under the care of New Brunswick Presbytery while at Princeton, and so was licensed in April, 1881, by that Presbytery.

The Church of Chester being vacant at that time, and

hearing various candidates, was supplied by Mr. Beattie for two Sabbaths, though not consciously as a candidate. The people were quite pleased with the young man, both in and out of the pulpit. A hearty call was extended to him and he began his labors with the Church on June 27th, 1882.

While serving the Church of Chester he was made Moderator of the Presbytery of Hudson. Since then he has served as the Moderator of Pueblo Presbytery, and twice also as the Moderator of the Presbytery of the Rio Grande, and has acted as the stated clerk of the latter Presbytery for seven years. He has also represented the several Churches and Presbyteries with which he has been connected, in the General Assembly.

The Church was in good condition when Mr. Beattie accepted the pastorate, and the numbers about as large as could be expected in Chester. All the services were well attended except the prayer meeting. The Sunday School, too, needed considerable attention as it always does, unless some godly man of executive ability has charge of it. These two branches of work called for special effort and thought. They had up to this time been conducted either in the audience room or in the basement of the Church. The latter was both gloomy and damp. Some of the people were afraid to attend prayer meetings in such a place. This led to the practical consideration of a new Chapel, which could be used for all such purposes. Pretty soon a subscription paper was started with the purpose of securing money enough to build a Chapel costing about $2,500. Sufficient encouragement was secured to warrant the going forward with the undertaking. But it was found that the ideas of the people were larger than the first design, so that the building, when complete, cost nearly $5,000. It is a beautiful and comfortable large Sunday School room with two primary departments in the rear.

With such commodious rooms the Chester congregation began to think of a large pipe organ as the next most necessary thing for their Church. This is what led Mr. Beattie to say "just a day or two before I started for Europe, we had some kind of an entertainment—I think a sociable, in the Chapel—and then we began the organ fund."

The organ, however, was not secured during his pastorate. After attending so effectively to the rear of the Church, Mr. Beattie turned his attention to the front, inviting the people to grade and make the beautiful lawn which we see today. Mr. Beattie was second to none in the execution of this work, laboring to level the soil and scatter the seed as vigorously as any of his parishioners.

However, he says he does not regret it, as it was the means of securing him Miss Ruby Miller, and they were married in the Chester Presbyterian Church July 28th, 1891.

The Church took on a new color on the outside, and new furnaces were placed in the cellar at his suggestion. The Parsonage lawn was reclaimed from its wilderness appearance by regrading and seeding it. In 1887, the congregation gave him a vacation of three months that he might visit Europe and get the great benefit that is always to be had in travel. He had gone only as far as Ireland when he was suddenly and quite unexpectedly taken with a hemorrhage of the lung that forced him to return immediately to America. This cut short his traveling in that direction, though he has visited Mammoth Cave, Ky., Alaska, Yellowstone Park, and Yosemite. Every year also he crosses the Continent twice, that he and his wife may visit their old home and their large circle of friends.

After a long sickness following his return from Europe, some months having been spent in the Adirondacks, and still a longer time at his father's home in Scotchtown, without any assurance of recovery from his lung trouble while in this climate, he at length resinged his charge at Chester. Forty-eight had been added to the Church during his short pastorate, and much good work had been set in motion.

Feeling strong enough to do some work late in the Summer of 1888, he took charge of the Presbyterian Church at Las Animas, Colorado. There he labored successfully until he was called to his present charge, the First Presbyterian Church of Albuquerque, New Mexico, in 1890. He accepted this charge on condition that it should withdraw from the board and be self-sustaining. This was done and the Church has struggled nobly with all these trying business years, and has succeeded, admirably, giving the Pastor as fine a house to live in as any parsonage in Orange Co.

During Mr. Beattie's sickness, and while he was still Pastor at Chester, the Rev. David Stevenson, D.D., supplied the pulpit for many Sabbaths. The Church, however, was desirous of a settled Pastor on whom it might rely for the building up of the Church in every direction.

Candidates were again invited and many were heard, when the Lord finally directed the much lamented and beloved Dr. Burrows to Chester.

Rev. John F. Burrows, D.D.

DR. BURROWS was called to the pastorate of the Chester Presbyterian Church, on May 2d, 1889, where he remained in the faithful performance of his duty until the Master called him home to glory, April 10th, 1894.

The Rev. John F. Burrows, D.D., was born at Arnold, in Nottinghamshire, England, December 25, 1831, and died in Chester, New York, April 10, 1894, in the 63rd year of his age. (Aged 62 years, 3 months and 15 days.)

His father, John Burrows, died before his recollection of him, leaving him an only child. His mother's brother, Thomas Burrows, came to this country a few years after, and, having made a home for himself in Philadelphia, sent for his sister, Sarah Burrows and her son John, then about twelve years old. Here they lived until about the year '57, when they removed to near Williamstown, Gloucester County, New Jersey, where the mother died about five years ago, and where the uncle still lives, an aged man.

His uncle was a manufacturer, but John loved his books and aspired to college. He finished his preparation in Wilmington, Del., in a school conducted by the Rev. Samuel M.

Gayley, a then famous teacher. He entered Lafayette College and was graduated with the class of '57. Having early made a profession of his faith in Christ, at the age of seventeen his heart was filled with a desire to preach to his fellow men the great salvation by which he himself was saved.

At intervals from his preparations for college to his graduation he had taught. For this avocation he was apt, and spent his first year out of college in the same employ in the Parocial school in Newton, Pa., under the principalship of the Rev. George Burrows, D.D., now Professor in the Theological Seminary in San Francisco, Cal. He entered Princeton Theological Seminary in '58, graduating in due course in '61. This fondness for teaching and his constant desire to be useful led him to have in his second charge a class of boys, in which several prepared wholly or in part for college, and of that number three are now in the Gospel ministry and one is a Christian physician.

Soon after completing his studies he accepted a call to the Second Presbyterian Church of Amwell, Hunterdon County, N. J., and was ordained and installed there by the Presbytery of Raritan, November 26, 1861. His first pastorate was a very happy one among an intelligent and appreciative people, and continued seven years until 1868, when he accepted a call to the Presbyterian Church at Milford, N. J., in the same county, where he remained five years, until 1873, winning universal and enduring esteem and confidence; when he accepted a call to the Third Presbyterian Church of Williamsport, Pa., where he labored faithfully and successfully for eleven years, until 1884.

He closed this his longest pastorate by accepting a call to Olean, N. Y. Here he continued the good citizen, the genial gentleman, the true friend, the wise counselor, the faithful Pastor, the eloquent preacher, until the latter part of the year 1889, when he accepted a call to the Presbyterian Church of Chester, N. Y., where for more than five years he has lived the same devoted Christian life and preached the same pure Gospel down to the day of his death.

A local paper says of him as Pastor of the Church of Chester, that the deepest affection and the greatest respect existed between him and the members of his congregation. He was sincerely beloved by rich and poor.

Perhaps no member of the Presbytery of Hudson did more preaching during the past six months on the plan of ministerial visitation instituted by the Presbytery September, 1893, and his quiet, persuasive earnestness is remembered with tender affection wherever he went.

He was a faithful student, carefully preparing his sermons, and an orthodox theologian, believing that the whole "Bible is the Word of God and the only infallible rule of faith and practice;" a scriptural preacher, knowing that this Word is able to save our souls; a loyal alumnus of his alma mater, which in the year 1886 conferred on him the degree of D.D.; an American citizen, true to all the institutions of his country in sentiment and expression—in a word, true and faithful and good in every relation of life, for words fail us to express our estimation of him as son, husband, father; surely, wherever he lived the Gospel of the Christian family was preached by example as well as by precept.

His wife, daughter and son were with him during his brief and painful illness until the end came, and he had "entered into his rest."

During his long ministry of a third of a century he had not been laid aside from work by illness; for the last month he had suffered from the grip, but had preached every Sabbath, omitting the evening service. His session urged him to take a vacation and allow them to supply the pulpit, and he promised them to do so soon.

It was too late. He had finished his course.

At the very beginning of his ministry, in 1861, he was married to Miss Clara Davis, the cultured daughter of Josiah Davis, Esq., of Easton, Pa. His family consisted of a son and daughter, who, with their mother and aunt are now living at Bethlehem, Pa.

During his ministry in Chester souls were gathered steadily into the Church, the Christian Endeavor Society was organized, the rotary system of Elders was introduced, and Gospel Services held in other places than the Church.

Five new Elders were added to the session at the beginning of his ministry. These were Alfred B. Roe, Samuel S. Durland, Chas. B. Roe, John N. Bernart and Thomas B. Roe. His was a splendid work well done, carried forward grandly from beginning to end. The last of his labors were not the least, for he sowed the seed more faithfully, possibly, in these last years than in any of all the preceding.

Rev. Robert Houston M'Cready, Ph.D.

THE present pastor was born July 12, 1853, in the city of Pittsburgh, Pennsylvania, and lived in that vicinity till he was seventeen years of age. His father died when he was about fourteen years old, and in that same year he began life for himself as a store boy, with the firm of Wagstaff & Bro., the grocers. He spent between three and four years serving customers with food for the body. He was away from home all week, but spent every Sabbath at home with his mother and two sisters. Before his father's death their Church fellowship had been with the New Light Covenanters, and the General Assembly Presbyterian Church. After his father's death, the family attended the Covenanter Church (Old Side), on 8th street, Pittsburgh, Rev. A. M. Milligan, D.D., Pastor.

At sixteen he made a public confession of faith and became a member of the Church. He had no thought of studying for the ministry at that time. But he became a firm believer in the Gospel of Christ as the saving power of society. He found in later life that the limitations of the Covenanter Church were too great and not required by the spirit or words of the New Testament as he reads it. He longed for greater liberty in bringing men to Christ.

When the call came to him to preach the Gospel if God opened the way, he left the store for the school. That step was taken very much against the wish of those of his own home. His business prospects were bright, and he was expected to take up the drug business that had been established in connection with the home by his father and other brothers. But after careful consideration and much prayer, the decision to go forward in the chosen calling was made. He resolved to go on until God blocked the way. More than once he thought it was blocked. Sickness touched one loved one after another, and they always looked to the student brother or son for help. When the way seemed hemmed in on every side, however, God opened some unexpected door and seemed to point onward.

He had received the average English education of the Public Schools of Alleghany City, Pa., where he was living from ten to fourteen years of age. Special advantages being offered him in a school of Antrim, Ohio, he studied under Prof. Love. Called home to attend to some financial matters, Rev. J. R. W. Sloane, D.D., Professor of Systematic Theology in Alleghany Seminary offered to fit him for College. He gladly accepted, and graduated from the Western University of Pennsylvania, Pittsburgh, Pa., in June, 1879.

One preparatory and three regular College years were spent in West Geneva College, Ohio, before entering the Western University of Pittsburgh, Pa.

During his College course he represented the Adelphic Literary Society successfully in three contests. The first was in recitation, the second in oration, the third in debate. He was also elected valedictorian of his class in the Western University where he graduated.

He went to the Theological Seminary the same year he graduated from College. He spent the required four years in the Alleghany Seminary, graduating in the Summer of 1883.

He received several calls, for there was a dearth of

preachers in the Church at that time. One to New Castle, Pa., another to New Concord, Ohio, where there was a United Presbyterian College. One to Oil City, Pa., and another to Barnesville, N. B. But he chose the call with the fewest members—Coldenham, N. Y. He was ordained and installed there March 6th, 1884. In 1887 he was called to a Church in Cincinnati. He declined that but accepted a call to the Prospect Hill Presbyterian Church the next year, in 82d street, near Park avenue, New York City. He remained with this Church until it was reunited with the First Union Congregation, from which it came out, and until he received a call to the Old Brick Church at Montgomery. This was in 1890. He was married to Belle H. Beattie, daughter of Rev. David Beattie, of Scotchtown, N. Y., while settled in New York, June 21, 1888.

When the call came from Montgomery Brick Church there was this strong plea added to the call, "it was the old home of Mrs. McCready." Her father's congregation joined this one on the North

While settled at Montgomery, Mrs. McCready's mother and father both died, which broke that tie to the place at least. The work in Montgomery was most successful. But all that it seemed possible for Mr. McCready to do was done, and this was more strongly impressed than ever when the call came from Chester, N. Y. It was not sought, and was indeed at first hardly listened to. But He who rules over all our lives brought us to Chester, where the lines have fallen unto us in pleasant places.

Shortly after Mr. McCready's coming to Chester, or early in 1895, a strong revival spirit seemed to be awakened among the people. As a result, the Rev. Arthur J. Smith, now pastor of the First Presbyterian Church of Atlanta, Georgia, was invited to conduct a series of meetings. The fruit of those meetings was very gratifying. About seventy souls were added to the Church, making nearly one hundred souls added since the present pastorate began.

Notwithstanding the fact that many have passed to the Church triumphant recently, the work of the Church has pushed vigorously forward in many directions.

The Christian Endeavor Society has been enlarged and taken on a new inspiration.

A Home Department Class, in connection with the Sabbath School work, has been started. It is under the supervision of Miss Carrie E. Durland, and is nearly as large as the Sabbath School proper.

A Teachers' Class has been established and a Ladies' Aid Society organized.

An elegant new parsonage and barn have been built on the Church grounds. It is a beautiful modern house with every convenience and enhances the whole Church property to a marvelous degree. New and beautiful opalescent windows have been put in the Church; the decorations on the inside have been renewed, and the entire building repaired and painted. New lamps have replaced the old ones and the light both by day and by night has been increased to the point of cheerfulness.

The century that is past has written a splendid Church record. This Church has marched near the front rank of the faithful, the aggressive and the spiritual churches of the land. It is marked by no rents or feuds.

Love is its watchword and its aim is to impart the character of the Son of God to every believer.

"This man and that man there" in all the walks of life points with pride to the Chester Church as his spiritual birthplace.

All the people round about have been enlightened and inspired by the Word of God faithfully preached and applied to their hearts by the power of the Holy Spirit.

The children rise up in gratitude to bless their parents for the precepts and principles, the liberties and privileges which they have handed down to them. Parents and children join the invisible Choir in singing songs of Praise to God for His goodness.

May thy children's children sing Praise to God for His goodness, O sons and daughters of Chester. May they sing forever in the New Jerusalem.

May "peace be within thy walls and prosperity within thy palaces."

SHOWING THE CHURCH AS DEDICATED IN 1854
SHOWING THE CHAPEL IN THE REAR, BUILT IN 1884.
SHOWING THE CHURCH AS REMODELED WITH MEMORIAL WINDOWS INSERTED IN 1898.

The Present Session of the Church.

REV. ROBERT H. McCREADY, *Moderator*.

Elders.

SAMUEL S. DURLAND, *Clerk*.

GABRIEL SEELY,   SAMUEL HADDEN,
WARREN HELMS,   JOSEPH DURLAND,
CHARLES B. ROE,   ALFRED ROE,
JOHN N. BERNART.   THOMAS B. ROE.

A List of Elders

IN THE FIRST PRESBYTERIAN CHURCH OF CHESTER, N. Y., FROM ITS UNION WITH THE PRESBYTERY OF HUDSON UNTIL THE PRESENT TIME.

Names.	Date of Election.	Died or Ceased to Act.
Seth Marvin,	April 15, 1813	Aug. 25, 1815
Jonathan Hallock,	" " "	Nov. 16, 1816
Wm. Vail,	" " "	*July 27, 1838
Elnathan Satterly,	Sept. 4, "	Oct. 19, 1836
Abraham Stickney,	" " "	Nov. 9, 1823
Joseph Sherwood,	Mar. 23, 1816	Dec. 4, 1838
Ebenezer Halbert,	" " "	*April 3, 1827
James Halbert,	Oct. 25, 1821	Sept. 30, 1871
Townsend Seely, M.D.,	" " "	*April 3, 1837
Eph. A. Beckwith,	Dec. 5, 1825	*April 4, 1831
Nat. H. Gale,	" " "	*April 25, 1833
Philo Gregory,	Aug. 21, 1835	*June 8, 1833
Nathaniel Rackett,	" " "	Mar. 13, 1840
John H. Tuthill,	" " "	*Mar. 11, 1847
Ira Hawkins,	May 5, 1839	May 12, 1871
Jesse Roe,	" " "	
G. S. Conklin,	" " 1843	*Jan. 4, 1872
Caleb C. Colwell,	" " "	*April 10, 1848
Seth M. Satterly,	Sept. 16, 1849	*Sept. 12, 1853
Nathaniel Roe,	" " "	Dec. 9, 1884
Narcus Sears,	" " "	Mar. 13, 1857
Gabriel Seely, Jr.,	April 9, 1858	Now acting.
Walter H. Conklin,	" " "	July 25, 1895
Jeheil A. Clark,	" " "	*Feb. 5, 1878
Robert W. Colfax,	" "	*April 5, 1887

George W. Clark,	Oct. 20, 1876	May 3, 1881
Samuel Hadden,	" " "	Now acting.
J. Warren Helms,	" " "	" "

The Rotary System of Eldership was adopted July 16th, 1889.

Alfred B. Roe,	July 16, 1889	Now acting.
Charles B. Roe,	" " "	" "
John N. Bernart,	" " "	" "
Thomas B. Roe,	" " "	" "
Samuel S. Durland,	" " "	" "
Joseph Durland,	" " "	" "

Sketches of the Elders.

All these whose sketches follow have been noble co-workers with the present Pastor with one exception.

Nathaniel Roe passed to his reward long before the present Pastor came. Walter H. Conklin shortly after he came. The sons of these worthy Elders have kept them with us in memorial windows, and a sketch of each is added to those of the living members of the Session. Other names will occur to you, such as Ira Hawkins, George S. Conklin, Jessie Roe, and R. W. Colfax as worthy of a place with these, but they must be left for a later time.

Samuel Hadden.

THE President of the village of Chester is a descendant, on his father's side, of the staunch French Huguenots, and on his mother's side of the persistent, truth-loving, God-fearing Scotch.

His parents, Bartholomew and Elizabeth Brown Hadden, lived at Narrowneck, near Rye, N. Y. They removed thence to Rockland Co., near Munsey's, where the subject of this sketch was born March 19th, 1828.

In 1846 he went to Vail's Gate to learn the carriage making trade. He was married March 7th, 1851, to Eliza J. Magill, and settled permanently in Chester in 1854.

He began the carriage-making business here in the same year, and soon won a wide reputation throughout this and other counties for the quality and style of his carriage building. There was strong competition, and many days during the civil war when people were more interested in cannon than in carriages, so that business was not brisk. But the skies cleared. The civil war had two effects upon his business. It lessened competition and increased the demand for carriages. As fortune influence and friends increased, he naturally took a greater interest in all that concerned the wellfare of Chester.

His personality has marked nearly every improvement about the Presbyterian Church of Chester. The present building was dedicated the same year in which he settled in Chester. This may account for his desire to see things about it to his liking. He wanted good sheds, and in a proper place. It was the same way in regard to securing the lecture room and the organ.

He has spared no pains in securing for the Church beautiful opalescent windows. The individuals and societies who paid for them as memorial tributes are more than gratified with the improvement they have made in the Church. About 1865 he was elected to the office of Trustee and served eleven years, or until he was made an Elder in 1876. He attended the General Assembly in 1882, and has been a delegate to Synod and Presbytery several times.

Mr. Hadden has served as the Supervisor of the town five terms, and also as Collector and Inspector.

Not averse to politics, yet fully persuaded that he seeks no office, he has had thrust upon him many honors. The last honor, which came to him unexpectedly, was his election to the Presidency of the village of Chester, in March, 1898. He is recognized as a successful, progressive citizen, advocating the introduction of our water system, good roads, trolley system, and whatever else will make for the material welfare of the village.

He is not lacking, either, in his interest in the spiritual welfare of the people. He constantly urges young and old to accept the Christ whose salvation is life eternal.

As to his home life, his companion still continues with him. None of the three children born in their home are with them. The eldest, Alice, married to Charles S. Wells, lives near Goshen. The next, Clara, married to E. D. Green, died in 1888; and the youngest, Ellen Eugenia, married to John B. Otis, lives between Chester and Florida, on her father's farm, known as the Seward farm. To these children who have gone out from his own home his love is ever increasing, as we would expect. He is in the fullest sense a loving man. Large, portly, politic, suave and genteel in address, he loves his home and all within. He loves his neighbors; he loves the town of Chester; he loves the Presbyterian Church; he loves pure and undefiled religion; he loves the poor and the prosperous; he loves money, and loves to do good with it; he loves music and ministers and manliness.

While he has been somewhat in politics—and always a Republican—he has kept a clean record, because he loved honesty and truthfulness and integrity.

Standing, as he does to-day, the chosen head of the community in which he lives, he represents the best element of municipal life in one of the staid villages of our American commonwealth.

Joseph Durland.

THE President of the Chester National Bank has been a resident of the village of Chester ever since he was born, and has been identified with most of its prominent interests. He is the son of Samuel S. and Amelia Vernon Durland, and was born in Chester, March 16th, 1832. With the exception of one year which he spent as clerk in store, he remained on the homestead farm until 1856. During the three years following this, he and his stepfather were engaged in the Chester Mills, which they had bought. In 1807 they sold this mill property and moved to the prominent business place which is now known far and wide under the name of J. Durland & Son. Mr. Durland was married to Miss Nancy Board, daughter of Jas. J. Board, February 25th, 1857, and became successor to his father-in-laws interest in the firm of Board, Pierson & Co. A new partnership was then formed with Thos. G. Pierson and Jas. R. Bell, and continued to do business under the name of Pierson, Bell & Durland. In February, 1862, the firm again changed, Mr. Durland retaining his place, but securing his brother, Samuel S., for a partner in place of the other two men. This partnership continued pleasantly for ten years, when his brother withdrew and left him sole proprietor of the business, which he continued until 1885. In the meantime there had been five children born in his home—James B., Frank, Amelia Vernon, Marion, and Nettie E. His son Frank became a recognized partner in the firm in 1885, which gives this business firm its present name, J. Durland & Son.

While Mr. Durland has steadily pushed his business in Chester, he has not been limited to that alone.

For a number of years he has been identified with the Savings Banks of both Goshen and Warwick, and has for twelve years been a director of the Chester National Bank.

It was not strange, therefore, at the death of its old and honored President, John T. Johnson, and in the long continued illness of its worthy Cashier, Jonas D. Millspaugh, that he should be called to the Presidency. He was elected to that position June 19th, 1897, and has since conducted the business of the bank with admirable skill.

His business enterprise and executive ability have been of great service to his native village in many ways. He was influential in establishing the present Union Free School; was a member of the first Board of Education and Clerk of the Board for seven years. He strongly urged the incorporation of the village of Chester in November, 1892, and was a member of its first Board of Trustees. Likewise in the matter of water supply for the village. He was a member and Secretary of the Board of Water Commission during the entire construction of the water works, and has the satisfaction of knowing that the water system is not surpassed in the State.

He has never taken an active part in anything but local politics, and the broader field, so far as it affected home interests. Two years in the office of Supervisor, which he held from 1866 to 1868, satisfied him with public political offices.

While he has been thus deeply interested in everything that concerns the welfare of the village and engrossed in many business interests, he has not forgotten entirely the work of the Master's Kingdom.

In 1855 he made a public confession of Christ and united with the Church under Dr. Wood.

He has been as anxious to see the Church grow as the village. He was made a Deacon in 1889, in which office he served until he was elected Elder in 1890. His position as a business man and his natural quality as a leader in business matters has enabled him to render much unseen and unrewarded service to the Church. He has collected the pew rents at his store for about twenty years ; has been a teacher for twenty-five years, and Superintendent and assistant Superintendent of the Sunday School. He is not an exhorter or Preacher, but an unconscious peacemaker and concilliator. He has joined hands with a few of his brethren in placing opalescent windows in the Church during this Centennial year, and stands ready for the next enterprise that will glorify God.

Gabriel Seely.

THE Seely family is one of the oldest and most numerous families in the vicinity of Chester. Gabriel Seely is one of its oldest members. He has the honor of being the oldest and possibly the most spiritual man in the present session of the Church. He was born August 10th, 1819, the same year as Queen Victoria. His life, however, has been spent in a much less conspicuous sphere. He began his life in the now spacious home of Mrs. Thaddeus Seely, his sister-in-law. He is the sixth child in a family of seven born to Thaddeus and Elizabeth Roe Seely, and was noted for his nervy, frolicsome boy life. He was not satisfied with the humdrum of farm life at first, but slowly settled down to make himself one of the most progressive farmers of his community.

His parents were bent on giving him the advantages of an education. He was sent to the public school at Summerville and Chester. Later he attended several academies, viz., the one at Florida, N. Y., the one at Montgomery, N. Y., under Prof. Tucker, and the academy at Ridgebury, N. Y., while the late Governor Bross was teaching.

He has attended service in all three of the Church buildings, pictures of which are to be found in this book. There was no railroad here when he was a boy and all the farm produce had to be driven to Cornwall, and shipped to New York by way of the Hudson. Some of the wood for the first steamboat was purchased of his father, and it is with deep interest that he looks back over the vast strides forward that have been made in his lifetime.

His childhood's home was not the most religious in Chester, and he was a little inclined to be worldly and reckless. But the Lord had another purpose in regard to him. In 1837 the Lord led Timothy Lester this way to assist Rev. Mr. Beach, then Pastor of the Chester Church, in conducting revival services. A very deep interest was awakened, and among those who accepted Christ and united with the Church, was Gabriel Seely.

He was married four years later, on September 9th, 1841, to Eliza Ann Gardner, daughter of Ira Gardner of Gardnersville, N. Y. One visit to the West satisfied him to remain in Orange Co.

In the year 1842 he moved into the now large well-furnished farm-house, where he lives, near Chester. It was quite small when he moved into it, but he has added to it as necessity demanded and means would permit.

There were six children born in the home. Two still abide with him and keep the home—Miss Martha Seely and Mrs. Belle Masterson, now a widow, and her only daughter Adele.

Mr. Seely, while an active man for one who has almost touched the threshold of the four score years, feels sorely the loss of his life companion, who died March 2nd, 1896.

While Mr. Seely has not been a great accumulator of money, he is recognized as one of the leading farmers in this part of the country. His farm is naturally a productive one and in Mr. Seely's palmy days held the first rank as a milk producing farm. Such a position is only won and held by hard labor and progressive investments in the latest improvements. During all these years Mr. Seely has not been idle in the Master's Kingdom. Quietly seeking with the Pastor in the secret chamber the outpouring of the Spirit and the Salvation of his fellow-men, he has witnessed many answers to his prayers.

Mr. Seely is a Republican in politics and a staunch advocate of temperance. So exemplary had his life been since uniting with the Church that he was elected to the eldership in 1858, in which relation he has served ever since with the greatest acceptance. He has attended the meeting of the New York Synod in Boston and Brooklyn, and has frequently represented the Church in other places. His interest in the Church was never greater than at present, though he is able to attend but little. His silvery locks and piercing eye lead you to think of the Elders that bow around the throne of the Lamb. He has been in the furnace of affliction.

"Adversity is the diamond-dust Heaven polishes its jewels with."

Joseph Warren Helms.

YOU would not think to meet him of a morning, that he had passed, by seven years, the three-score and ten. He has faced much adversity, but it would seem that he could make John Wesley's language his. "I feel and grieve, but by the grace of God I fret at nothing." "Anxiety never successfully bridged over any chasm."

"'Tis always morning somewhere, and above
The awakening continents, from shore to shore,
Somewhere the birds are singing evermore."

But this man has faith that the angels are singing overhead. He believes that the loved ones who have gone on before, are waiting till he comes. He believes that all defects are hidden by the robe of Christ's righteousness and that men are loved for their faith, not for their works. This shows the man a solid, doctrinal, loyal Christian, loving the Presbyterian Church as the proper body of Christ on the earth.

He was the oldest of seven children born to Nathan W. and Julia Ann Marvin Helms. The two sons of this family are still living. They are retired farmers. His brother, Nathan H. Helms, lives with the only surviving sister, Mrs. Woodhull, at Oxford Depot, N. Y., and looks after his farm which is not far distant. The subject of our sketch makes his home with his children, spending the Sabbath especially with his son Nathan in Chester, while the rest of the time is spent with his daughter Ruth, at Monroe, N. Y.

He was born in the town of Blooming Grove, not far from Grey Court, July 27, 1820. He is, therefore, the second eldest of the members of the session of Chester Church.

His education was secured in the public school at Oxford, later he attended school at Newburgh, and later still at Blooming Grove, N. Y. Whether he ever had thoughts of any other calling than that of farming, is not known. He is so well acquainted with the points of Church law, that it would seem as if he had a natural aptitude for law. He has served the public for six years as Commissioner of Highways in the town of Blooming Grove from 1867 to 1873. He had also served the public in the Civil War by voluntarily sending a substitute to the front when he could not go himself.

He remained on the home farm with his parents until about 26 years of age, when he was married to Miss Elizabeth Roe, daughter of Lewis H. Roe, of Monroe.

He and his bride began their life of hope and toil and joy near Oxford Depot, N. Y. Three children were born to them, Ruth, Mary and Nathan. They all grew to maturity, but Mary died, unmarried, January 30th, 1897, after a long illness. Her spirit, however, was ripe for the Master's call. She passed from the vision of many friends, much loved, much lamented, with strong assurance that she would "see the King in his beauty and the land of very far vision."

All the children had united early in life with the Chester Church, doing better even than their father in this respect, since he put it off until he was about thirty-five. But he was so well equipped when he did unite with the Church in the qualities that make an elder that he was elected to that position in Monroe two years after accepting Christ.

He served that Church with Rev. Dr. Daniel N. Freeland for nineteen years as an elder. Removing to Chester, he was elected to the eldership of this Church in 1876. He has served both churches well and represented his church with honor at the New York Synod in Elmira and New York City.

He is well known at Presbytery, where he has attended frequently. He is a man rich in feeling. He is strong in his likes and dislikes. He is in no sense a politician. He is a straightforward citizen of the highest Christian type. His love for his children is very marked. Modest in regard to his own distinguishing qualities, he believes that his wife, who died in 1884, has left such a legacy of love, loyalty, purity and Christian benevolence to their children as seldom falls to the lot of any home.

Even the grandchildren have caught the spirit of this noble grandmother in Israel and labor incessantly for the building up of the Master's kingdom.

"Love is the fulfilling of the law."—Romans xiii: 10.

Samuel S. Durland.

HE was the eldest son of James and Amelia Vernon Durland, and was born January 21st, 1840, in Chester. He sits, not in the old house but in the old homestead, to read the family Bible in the very spot where he first saw the light. When asked where he was born, he pointed to a spot in the dining room and said "right here."

His surroundings indicate the man of thrift, good judgment and genial living that you find him on long or short acquaintance. He is a thorough accountant and penman and has been identified with William A. Lawrence in the manufacture of Neufchatel and Cream Cheese. This is the most extensive factory of the kind in the United States, and is located on Mr. Durland's old homestead farm. Mr. Durland has been connected with this factory since 1879, and it has a constantly increasing trade.

His education was all obtained in Chester Free School and Academy, except what he gained in a brief term in Bloomfield, N. J. When twenty-one years of age he left the home farm for a brief period and went into the general merchandise store of Tuthill & Aeger at Warwick, N. Y. The way was open and strong inducements led him to give up business in Warwick and return to Chester.

His brother Joseph having bought out the interest of Belle & Pierson, who had been in partnership with him for five years, persuaded his brother Samuel to go into business with him where the firm of J. Durland & Son is now located.

This pleasant business relation continued with his brother for ten years, or until 1872, when he sold out and returned to the old homestead farm.

He was married while associated with his brother in business in Chester. The record reads, "Nov. 6th, 1867, Samuel S. Durland was united in marriage to Margaret T. Seely, by the Rev. Thomas Nichols, at the home of the bride." Two children have been born to them, Selah S. and Jane T., both of whom are still living at home with their parents.

He confessed Christ publicly and united with the Church in May, 1873. He has been serving this Presbyterian Church with which he has grown up, for more than a quarter of a century, in some relation or other. In 1889 he was elected to the eldership, and for the last three years has been serving most acceptably as the Clerk of Session.

Modest, spiritual, generous, sincere, peace-loving, he has sought no political favors. But as a loyal citizen and christian gentleman he has sought to do his whole duty, to both church and state, a man to whom Chester is proud to point as a son of the soil of Chester.

Alfred B. Roe.

THE Roe family is very large in Chester, and Alfred B. is the direct descendant of one of the oldest branches in the town. He is of Scotch descent, the family having come from that country in 1730, and settled in Florida, N. Y.

The old homestead on which Alfred B. lives, now in the town of Chester, was purchased in 1751, and has continued to be the home of this branch of the Roe's ever since.

Alfred B. Roe was one of a family of seven children born to Jesse and Dolly Caroline Booth Roe. He began his career August 12, 1840, in one of the typical luxurious homes of this beautiful valley.

He was provided with the best schooling which Chester could afford, and finished his course in Bloomfield, N. J.

He allowed nothing to divert him from farming. No other calling had quite so much charm for him. If he ever thought of law, or theology, or medicine, or business, or the army as a calling, something came to prevent his entering upon any of these lines of life. He seemed destined to farm, and is satisfied with his destiny. In any other line he might have been a success, but in farming he is a grand success.

He has been an ardent Republican from his earliest

political associations, and is justly proud of what his party has achieved in the history of our nation. While aspiring to no place of political power and emolument, he is deeply interested in filling all offices with good and true men.

He was married February 25th, 1869, to Miss Martha V. Durland. They began their married life on the home farm, but in a new house which was built for the young couple.

Five children were born to them, one of which died in infancy. Three of the others are still living at home, Jesse, Miss Anne and Fred, while the oldest daughter, Matilda, is married to Dr. H. B. Masten and lives in the village of Chester. Alfred B. Roe united with the Church when he was fifteen years of age, at the time of special ingathering after the erection of the present Church building.

He is, therefore, while still a young man, one of the oldest members of the Presbyterian Church of Chester. It seemed very fitting that he should be elected, as he was in 1889, to the Eldership, after serving as Trustee for ten years, and a member of the Church for thirty-four.

He has represented the Church at Presbytery, has served as a member of the Board of Education for ten years, and as a Director of the Chester National Bank since 1894.

A deep sorrow has fallen upon his household in the unexpected death of his beloved wife in February, 1896. She had been a wife and mother in the truest sense of those words, and was the inspiration upward of all who knew her.

Charles Board Roe.

MR. ROE was one of a family of six children born to Nathaniel and Sarah Board Roe. Their house was located on a rugged, sightly hillside near Oxford Depot, N. Y., where he was born March 25th, 1844.

Here he grew to manhood with his four brothers, Gabriel Seely, Thomas Beach, Nathaniel, Henry Martyn, and one sister, Hannah Elizabeth, who died November 29th, 1884. The old homestead still remains in the family, and is enjoyed by his brother, Thomas Beach.

The little school-house at Oxford Depot was a great factor in the small boys life in his day, and Charles was a faithful student, not only here, but at the Chester academy, where he was prepared for college by Prof. Edward Orton, the then famous teacher in the village of Chester.

Amherst seems to have been the popular college among the young men of his community in the sixties, from which institution we find him graduating with great credit in 1866.

He began teaching the next Fall in Ohio. But the locality so affected his health, and especially his eyes, that he was compelled to return to Orange County, N. Y. Having had exceptional privileges and training in one of the most staunch Christian homes of the community, it is not surprising that we find him making a confession of faith and uniting with the Church at the early age of thirteen.

The Rev. James W. Wood, D.D., having been the beloved Pastor of the Presbyterian Church for many years, was much gratified to receive this young disciple, with many others, during the revival of 1857-1858.

It is worthy of note that he acknowledges, in addition to the parental and pastoral instruction, the influence of a faithful public school teacher in leading him to accept Christ. He was married December 30th, 1886, to Miss Allie Stephens, of Salem, N. Y., and has established himself amid the rugged hills of his birth in a beautiful modern home, adjacent to the old homestead, near Oxford Depot, N. Y. His farm is a spacious one, and lies in the line of the Chester water pipes from Walton lake. He may at any time have all the benefits of a suburban residence, with steam heat and hot and cold water in all parts of the house. His home is a happy one, though it has in it only the prattle of one little adopted daughter—Helen.

He has served two terms as the Trustee of his school district, and five years the Superintendent of the Chester Presbyterian Sunday School, and has been for many years an active worker in the religious society of Oxford Depot. He was chosen an Elder in the Presbyterian Church of Chester—first in 1889, and again in 1895, in which office he still continues to serve with great acceptance to the people.

Scholarly, earnest, strong in his open testimony for Christ, he is the faithful, devoted, benevolent, genial disciple, friend and brother that you would expect to find as the result of such a training.

Thomas Beach Roe.

IS the brother of Charles B. Roe, and was born near Oxford Depot, N. Y., 1847. He had all the influences of a Christian home from his earliest infancy. But in addition to that, all the children of Nathaniel and Sarah Board Roe were taught diligence, frugality, honesty and love for the Church.

Born in the house where he now lives, though it has had many additions since then, he moved with his parents, in 1855, to the homestead now occupied by his brother Henry. He left his father's house to take up work for himself on the old homestead in 1869, and has made that his home ever since.

After having lived for fifteen years in his modest bachelor way with his brother Charles B. and sister Hannah E. as companions, he persuaded a pretty little school teacher, Miss Elizabeth Pearsall Gaunt, to become his wife, May 15th, 1884. She is the daughter of Delaplain and Penelope Gaunt, and her mother still lives with her. She is as remarkable a woman as his mother, and has proved herself in every way the companion he needed. She is intelligent, capable, thrifty, sincere, benevolent, earnest and deeply spiritual. She is a thoroughly consecrated, genial woman. They have two children living. William and Thomas B., their eldest having died when five years of age with that dreaded disease—diptheria.

In addition to the school privileges which Oxford Depot afforded, Mr. Roe had the benefit of the noted schools at Chester, Cooperstown, N. Y., and East Hampton, Mass.

He was received into the Church at the early age of ten years by the beloved Pastor of the Chester Presbyterian Church, Rev. James W. Wood, during a series of special meetings in 1857 and 1858.

Mr. Roe's vocation is that of a dairy farmer. He has evidently been quite successful in it, as the little house of his father's has grown to be quite a spacious residence with all the modern improvements and conveniences. It is thoroughly heated with steam radiators, and is supplied with water from the Chester water main. The barn, too, is supplied with water from the same source, and has every facility connected with it for making the dairy profitable.

Mr. Roe has by nature a strong religious character, which has been faithfully cultivated and is thoroughly reliable. He attends religious service in all kinds of weather and under all circumstances. And while not gifted in the art of oratory, he is always willing to testify his love for Christ and lead the people to God in prayer.

He was elected Elder in 1889, and has served the Church most faithfully in that relation ever since.

Quiet, unassuming, steadfast as the Scotch granite character from which he has sprung, he is recognized as one of the pillars of the Church which he so generously and willingly sustains.

John N. Bernart.

THE youngest elder in our Church at the present time, has an ancestry of which he is worthily proud. Born at Boardville, N. J., December 9th, 1860, where his mother's family had lived for several generations, he has no difficulty in tracing his blood back to the staunch inhabitants of Wales. Several of his ancestors by the name of Board crossed the Atlantic and settled in that section of New Jersey which has taken its name from the family — Boardville. On his father's side he claimed descent from the hardy, persevering broad-breasted lovers of liberty who came to this country from the Netherlands.

His father, Rev. James Elmendorf Bernart, was born at Millstone, N. J., March 15, 1821. He was educated at Rutgers College and Seminary, both of which institutions are under the control of the Dutch Reformed Church. He was graduated from the college in 1848 and from the Seminary three years later. His second pastorate, which covered a period of twenty-five years, was spent in Boardville, N. J. It was there that he met and married Miss Elizabeth Board, sister of Mrs. Nathaniel Board Roe. J. N. Bernart's father has always been a loyal member of the Dutch Reformed Church.

"Hence," says Mr. John Bernart, "I was born and reared in the Dutch Reformed Church, and my spiritual nature nourished and fed on the Heidelburgh Catechism. My early education was secured in the district school of Boardville, N. J., and it must have been of the very best quality, for my father was at that time the teacher of the school. My father having prepared me for college, I entered Rutgers, of New Brunswick, N. J., in my 18th year. I took the scientific course to fit myself for civil engineering, and spent three busy and profitable years in my Alma Mater, working for a diploma. But I had another thought in my mind which was stronger than that of civil engineering, and which I had cultivated from childhood—that of agriculture."

The fascination of the green hills and grassy meadows grew upon him till at length, in 1881, the family bought their present farm. The family at that time consisted of father, mother, sister and brother. He was converted during his last year in college, largely through the earnest prayers of his mother, followed up with a loving letter. As he read those earnest, entreating words and looked up into the face of Christ, he was forever melted and resolved to accept the salvation which Christ was so freely offering, and he united with the Reformed Church of New Brunswick, N. J. In 1881 he united with the Chester Church by letter, and in 1889 was elected a ruling elder, in which office he still continues.

Mr. Bernart is recognized as a very efficient church worker. He is the Clerk of the congregation and had been either Superintendent or Assistant Superintendent of the Sabbath School for more than ten years, or since 1886. A little abrupt in manner among young children, his strong sympathy and sincere desire to do good at all times is fully appreciated by all as existing beneath this exterior. Deeply spiritual, honest and strong in his convictions, a staunch temperance advocate, a conscientious citizen, a loyal Dutch-Presbyterian, he is appreciated and loved by all the people.

Nathaniel Roe.

IS known throughout the Church as "The Elder." His sacred memory is kept before those who knew and loved him, by his faithful children's tribute of a memorial window in the Chester Presbyterian Church.

He was recognized by all who knew him as a man worthy of being an elder in that Church. He is known as the man of God who went about doing good.

He was the eldest son of William and Mittie Mapes Roe, born November 11th, 1815, and showed his Scotch blood in his rugged character. Owing to the death of his parents he went, at the early age of eight years, to live with his grandfather, Thaddeus Seely, and after his death, lived with his son Gabriel Seely, in Chester. His wife, Sarah Board Roe, who still lives with her son Henry, was of as notable a family as her husband. She was the daughter of General Charles Board and Joanna Seely, and was born January 7th, 1815, at Boardville, N. J. She was the granddaughter of Joseph Board, who with his two brothers, James and David, emigrated from Wales and settled at that place, where they had charge of the iron works and owned some fifteen hundred acres of land—in Pompton Valley. She and her husband, who were of the same age, began housekeeping at the old homestead, near Oxford Depot, in 1843, immediately after their marriage, which took place on April 1st of that year. Here their six children—five sons and one daughter—were born. The daughter, Hannah E., died in 1884.

In 1855 they left the farm now occupied by their son, Thomas B., moving to the new farm now occupied by their son Henry, and where Mrs. Roe still lives. They began life with moderate means, but by 1867 they had by their frugality and thrift gathered together enough to warrant them in building the spacious and substantial residence on this new farm and in sight of the Grey Court Depot. Mrs. Roe is recognized by all as a very modest, retiring woman, but a faithful, intelligent, Christian mother, wife, friend and neighbor. Her large benevolence is well attested every year by her gifts to Missions and all worthy causes of the Church. The children show the stamp of their mother's character in godliness, upright dealing and careful business management. The sons say of her that "she dealt out the Catechism for heart and mind, as well as the slices of bread for the body, and they rise up and call her blessed." Mr. Roe was given a liberal common school education and was trained from his infancy in the principles of Christianity. Very regular in his attendance on divine ordinances he was converted in the prime of manhood; was chosen to the eldership while quite a young man, September 16, 1849, and served in that relation for thirty-five years, or until his death, December 9th, 1884.

He was of a quiet, retiring disposition, very kind as a husband, exemplary as father in his home, energetic and decisive in business. His children realized that his word was law, and while not stern, he was firm and decided. His was a home in which the family altar appeared in a strong light. Night and morning thanks were offered to God for all His goodness. The pastor and the flock were not forgotten, nor were the poor or the godless. He was a man of large sympathies, but not demonstrative. There was a sincerity in his utterance and such a kindly heartiness in his doing that his words always carried weight with them.

He was a Democrat in politics and served the Town of Chester three years as its assessor, representing it also in 1877 in the Board of Supervisors. His business ability was recognized by his neighbors, and he was made one of the directors of the Chester National Bank in 1879, in which position he continued till his death.

His falling asleep at the threshold of three score years and ten has probably been felt by the Church of which he was a member, and the poor of the community, more than that of any other man who has passed away in the last quarter of a century. But Christ was more real to them because this man had lived with them and had showed Him to them.

While the loved ones mourn and wait, they are assured that he who taught them how to believe in Christ is waiting for them.

Walter H. Conklin.

HE is known as the faithful Clerk of Session. His memory is honored by his son, Restcom P., with a memorial window in the Presbyterian Church of Chester.

He was the son of Benjamin and Mehitable Conklin, born May 20th, 1820, in Conklin town, near Goshen. His father and mother had both died before he was twelve years of age, and he went to live with his brother, Daniel Conklin, near Warwick, a man of great prominence in Chester in his day. He attended the public school at Warwick, and worked on his brother's farm until old enough to do for himself.

Not having full use of one arm owing to an injury sustained when a mere boy, he thought best to seek for lighter work than that of the farm. He engaged with John B. Randolph, the leading tailor of Warwick. Having served his apprenticeship, he sought for a wider field in which to ply his trade. New York offered the best opportunities to a young man and he located there, but the competition was very great.

While at work in New York he met a merchant from Amsterdam, N. Y., who persuaded him to go to that city and establish a business for himself. Accordingly he went to Amsterdam, in 1838, and opened a merchant tailoring store, and for five years carried on quite a successful business.

It was here that he met his companion in life, Miss Lucretia Chamberlin, a most remarkable woman and Church worker, and was married in 1842. He was at this time a young man of about twenty-two years of age, thoughtful, sincere, religious—seeking fellowship with the people of God. He and his wife united with the Presbyterian Church of Amsterdam, under Dr. Goodale. Strong inducements were held out to him to return to the vicinity of his old home, and seek to build up a business in Orange County. In 1843 he came to Chester, and established a fine trade as a merchant tailor.

Six children were born in the house, two of whom still survive—Restcom P., who occupies the old homestead in Chester, and is one of the honored and successful men of the village; and Mrs. Jennie E. Brooks, who has a beautiful home at Washingtonville, N. Y.

He was elected an Elder in the Presbyterian Church in 1858, and two years later was made Clerk of the Session, which position he held constantly until the time of his death. He had thus been closely associated with six Pastors, and knew many of the Ministers in the Presbyterian Church. He was twice sent by the Church to the General Assembly, and represented the Presbytery and Session many times at Synod. He had never aspired to political preferment, and was always satisfied to work for the good of his fellow men in the Church militant, that he might be the better fitted for the glorious call to the Church triumphant. His death on July 25th, 1895, was a sad blow to his companion in life, and was deeply felt by all who knew him.

The Present Board of Deacons.

H. M. Roi.

Ira Green.

C. E. Johnson.

"The poor ye have always with you." While you break the bread to them you will, Stephen like, instruct them. "Idleness is paralysis." Poverty is no virtue. "Blessed is the man who keeps out of the hospital and holds his place in the ranks," and yet, and yet, "ye have the poor always with you."

The Board of Trustees.

1898.

FRANK DURLAND, .	*President.*
JESSE ROE, ...	*Secretary.*
EDWARD D. GREEN,	*Treasurer.*
FRANK DURLAND, . .	. 1896
FRED. L. CONKLIN,	1898
EDWARD D. GREEN,	. 1896
JESSE ROE, . . .	1897
B. C. DURLAND,	1897
JOE Y. DAVIS, .	. 1898

The President, Frank Durland, superintends the renting of pews, and receives the pew rent at his place of business.

The Congregation meets annually on the last Tuesday of March for the transaction of business and the election of Trustees.

The annual meeting of the Congregation for the election of Elders and Deacons occurs on the second Tuesday of September.

GEORGE BARTOW, .   *Sexton.*

Trustees
In the Centennial Year.

Frank Durland.

E. D. Green.

E. L. Conklin.

Jno. V. Davis.

E. C. Durland.

Jesse Roe.

Trustees

During the Present Pastorate.

Fred. Selly.

Fred Vollmer.

James Selly.

James H. Roe.

Wm. Johnson.

The Women's Missionary Society

This is probably the most thorough working society of the Church. In response to an invitation to the ladies of the congregation to remain after the prayer meeting one evening in March, 1880, a beginning was made, with earnest thought and prayer, opening a way to organize a Women's Missionary Society.

Our Hudson Presbyterial Society had its birth, as well as our own, in the basement room of this Church, the mother society preceding our organization by one day, making the way clear to us.

On the 18th of March, 1880, we were regularly organized by Miss Loring, a returned missionary from Syria, with the thirty-seven following names as members:

Mrs. T. A. Leggett,
" Lucretia Conklin,
" Mary A. Wood,
" Sarah Roe,
" James M. Bull,
" George Seely,
" William Vail,
" Ely Conklin
" D. A. Conklin,
" G. F. Andrews,
" Harmon Showers,
" Harriet Brown,
Miss Lizzie Howell,
" Mary King,
" Helen King,
" Lizzie King,
" Hattie Kinner,
" Kate A. Vankleek,

Miss Emily Andrews.
" Amelia Andrews.
" Sarah Andrews,
" Lizzie Board,
" Bell Clark,
" Phebe Durland,
" Mame Durland,
" Carrie R. Durland,
" Emma Duryea,
" Libbie Duryea,
" Allie Duryea,
" Cornelia Edmondston,
" Ruth M. Everts,
" Francis W. Leggett,
" Hannah Roe,
" M. Belle Seely,
" Mattie A. Seely,
" Mary Seely,

Miss Julia Seely.

Having Mrs. Theodore A. Leggett for President, Miss

Mary King, Vice-President; Miss Carrie R. Durland, Secretary; Miss Hannah Roe, Treasurer.

Miss Loring's words of helpful direction counseling to open our meetings with prayer seemed almost beyond our ability. Does not this spiritual condition make known the need of a missionary society for ourselves? But our object was to work and pray in connection with other societies in the Presbytery of Hudson, to aid the Women's Home and Foreign Mission Boards of New York in sending out missionaries and sustaining them in their work.

At the end of the first year our membership had grown to the number of fifty, which number we held for several years. In passing time many of these members have moved away, twelve have been called home by the Master, while others have taken up the work. Our membership at present numbers thirty-eight, having for President, Miss Carrie R. Durland; 1st Vice-President, Mrs. R. H. McCready; 2d Vice-President, Mrs. F. B. Seely; 3d Vice-President, Mrs. Henry M. Roe; Secretary, Miss Belle Seely; Treasurer, Miss Jane T. Durland.

We have given to be used in mission work $3,000, an average of $166 per year. Only the Master knoweth in what spirit and how near it reaches the measure He has set.

The King's Daughters.

The Society was organized in 1898. It is not in any sense denominational, but was brought into existence through the great necessity which the Presbyterian Church felt in relation to the unsystematized charity work of the community.

Mrs. Helen B. Seely, President.
Mrs. Anna R. Pennoyer, Secretary.
Miss Josie Thompson, Assistant Secretary.
Mrs. Theodore Masterson, Treasurer.

There are nine committees, each with a separate line of work. All work is reported at each monthly meeting.

The Sunday School.

Jesse Roe,	Superintendent.
John N. Bernart,	Assistant.
Gertrude Huysler,	Secretary.
Emanuel F. Kallina.	Treasurer.
Albert Vollmer,	Librarian.
Mack T. Miller,	Librarian.

Primary Department.

Amelia C. Andrews,	Superintendent.

Teachers.

Miss Phebe Miller, Anna M. King, Mrs. Belle S. Masterson, Belle Seely, Amelia V. Durland, Marion Durland, Dolly Helms, Myra C. Roe, Mary Roe, Mrs. Ethel B. Barringer, Emanuel F. Kallina.

The Choir.

Miss Jane T. Durland,	Director.
Mr. Wm. B. King,	Organist.

Volunteer Chorus.

The Sacraments.

The Lord's Supper is observed on the first Sabbath of February, May, August and November.

Baptism will be administered on any Lord's Day by appointment.

The Ladies' Aid Society.

Mrs. Fred. B. Seely, ... *President.*
Mrs. Frank Durland, . *Secretary and Treasurer.*

Miss Katie Roe, Miss Jennie T. Durland, Mrs. W. J. Pennoyer, Miss Anna Seely, Mrs. George Seely, *Committee.*

Young People's Society of Christian Endeavor.

The Society was organized in 1889, and has for its aim the helping of the Church, the spiritual development of the youth of the Church, and the seeking of God's glory in doing His work on the earth.

The Junior Endeavor Society.

It grew out of the revival of 1895, and is now recognized as one of the best and largest societies in the county.

Mrs. Isabell H. M'Cready, . *Superintendent.*

THE PARSONAGE.

The Parsonage.

The Parsonage is an elegant modern house and unsurpassed by any manse in this part of the State. About the time of the settlement of the present Pastor there was assurance given that a new parsonage would be built. The resolution took definite form at a meeting of the congregation, held March 26th, 1895.

Work was immediately begun upon a good prospective plan, and the house was ready for occupancy November 1st, 1895.

Contract price, with appointments,	$6,695.58
Barn, grading, service pipes, etc.,	1,150.98
Total,	$7,846.56
Paid on parsonage,	4,924.51
Balance of account unpaid,	$2,922.05

The Building Committee whose personnel stamps the "manse" they have erected: are:

CHARLES R. BULL.   HENRY M. ROE.

Names of Members 1898.

Andrews, Geo. F.
Andrews, Mary Elizabeth
Andrews, Emily
Andrews, Amelia C.
Andrews, Elvira R.
Bachman, Mrs. Mamie
Bailey, Virginia
Bailey, Laura
Bailey, Lily
Banker, Geo. F.
Bennett, William H.
Bennett, Margaret S.
Bennett, May
Bernart, John N.
Bernart, Mary
Bernart, Charles
Board, J. Hudson
Board, Mary Elizabeth
Board, Martha S.
Board, Lizzie
Board, Wicks Seely
Board, Mary D.
Brya , Thomas H.
Bryan, Martha T.
Bulmer, Mary A.
Bull, Charles R.
Bull, Harriet R.
Bull, Caroline R.
Bull, Mary M.
Bull, Ann Elizabeth
Bull, Cornelia F.
Bull, Albert C.
Bull, Charles Ira
Bull, Mary Libbie
Bull, Mrs. Phœbe H.
Burrows, Mrs. Clara D.
Burrows, John F.

Bryan, David
Beach, John
Barringer, John F.
Barringer, Ethel B.
Barton, Mrs. Hannah A.
Carpenter, Dr. S. G.
Carpenter, Lizzie
Carpenter, Mrs. Harriet
Carpenter, Elizabeth
Carpenter, Olive
Clark, Jehiel G.
Clark, Carrie
Clark, Mrs. John
Clark, Martin J.
Clark, John H.
Conklin, Mrs. Dolly Ann
Conklin, Caroline
Conklin, William R.
Conklin, Phebe D.
Conklin, Fred L.
Conklin, Effie V. V.
Conklin, Mrs. Lucretia
Conklin, Rescomb P.
Conklin, George
Conklin, Alice S.
Conklin, Eli S.
Conklin, Phebe D.
Cornelius, Mrs. Harriet
Cornelius, Lizzie T.
Courter, Edna
Conklin, Ruth Pilgrim
Conklin, James H.
Conklin, Mrs. James H.
Davis, Mrs. Josephine
Davis, Mrs. Julia Ann
Davis, Mrs. Julia Bull
Decker, Mrs. Mary K.

Decker, Emily J.
Decker, Francis Amelia
DuBois, Mrs. Mary Emma
DuBois, Nettie May
Dunning, Mrs. C. Keziah
Dunning, Edith
Durland, Joseph
Durland, Nancy K.
Durland, Amelia Vernon
Durland, Marion
Durland, Nettie E.
Durland, James B.
Durland, Sarah A.
Durland, Frank
Durland, Mary S.
Durland, Samuel
Durland, Margaret
Durland, Jennie T.
Durland, Oscar
Durland, Matilda
Durland, Carrie Roe
Durland, Henry R.
Durland, Miss Mary E.
Durland, Martha
Durland, Nellie
De Groat, Louis
Davis, Alice
Davey, Miss Jesse
Durland, Mrs. E. Mapes
Earles, Mrs. Anna
Edmonson, Mrs. Drusilla D.
Edmonson, Cornelia
Edwards, Samuel
Edwards, Betsy
Edsall, Mrs. Eugenia
Farley, Azuba
Farley, Sarah E.
Foster, Mrs. Sarah J.
Gorham, Mrs. Elizabeth
Green, Mrs. Mary
Green, Lavinia
Green, Phebe
Green, Charles H.

Green, Huldah B.
Green, Edward D.
Green, Ira
Green, Alida
Green, Mamie Ethel
Green, Frederick A.
Green, William R.
Green, Mrs. Phebe B.
Green, Albert
Hadden, Samuel
Hadden, Eliza Jane
Helme, Warren
Helme, Nathan
Helme, Mary C.
Helme, Dolly
Helme, Mabel
Holbert, Mrs. Jessie
Houston, Joel
Howland, Mrs. Mary W.
Howland, Anna Louise
Hulse, Mrs. Charles
Huyster, Urban T.
Huyster, Mrs. Urban T.
Huyster, Gertrude E.
Huyster, Louise C.
Hyatt, Mrs. Myra
Jackson, Ezra T.
Jackson, Margaret D.
Johnson, Charles Ebenezer
Johnson, William
Kallina, Emanuel F.
Kallina, Anna
Kallina, Emanuel John
Kallina, Emma Tillie
King, Phebe B.
King, Debbie Ann
King, Edmund
King, Sarah
King, Helen M.
King, Lizzie D.
King, Anna M.
King, Mattie E.
King, Emma

Kinner, Miss Hattie
Latham, Mrs. Helen A.
Mapes, George H.
Mapes, Clara
Mapes, Grace Hamilton
Mapes, S. Elizabeth
Masterson, Mrs. M. Bella
Masterson, Fannie Adele
Miller, Mrs. Grey
Miller, May S.
Miller, Julia Case
Miller, Mack Taylor
Miller, Charles A.
Miller, Emma C.
Masten, Lillie
Masten, Lizzie
Millspaugh, Jonas D.
Millspaugh, Clara C.
Murray, Justus
Miller, Ida H., Miss.
McCready, Isabella
Odle, Miss Martha
Odell, Miss Nancy
Otis, Mrs. Elizabeth
Otis, Mary
Otis, Clara
Otis, Lona
Otis, Estella
Otis, John
Otis, Eugenia
Olmstead, Mrs. Hannah E.
Penoyer, William J.
Penoyer, Anna R.
Peterson, Thomas
Peterson, Maggie
Pilgrim, Mrs. Caroline
Pope, Mrs. Eliza B.
Powell, Mrs. Hannah
Price, Mrs. Elizabeth S.
Razey, James S.
Razey, Ethel D.
Roe, Alfred B.
Roe, Jesse N.

Roe, Amelia D.
Roe, Mrs. Sarah
Roe, Charles B.
Roe, Alfretta
Roe, Thomas B.
Roe, Elizabeth G.
Roe, Henry M.
Roe, Mrs. George M.
Roe, Helene S.
Roe, Mrs. Emily Colfax
Roe, Myra C.
Roe, Mary
Roe, Mrs. Mary
Roe, Mrs. Emily Cowdrey
Roe, Alfred B., Jr.
Roe, Mrs. Elizabeth
Roe, Kate Delano
Redner, Ruth Jane
Ross, Helen
Satterly, Millie
Seely, Mrs. Esther
Seely, Emma
Seely, Gabriel
Seely, Mary Ann
Seely, Martha A.
Seely, David R.
Seely, Julia Anna
Seely, Clara
Seely, Belle D.
Seely, Fred. B.
Seely, Ruth D.
Seely, Howard
Seely, Julia Youngs
Seely, Floyd
Seely, George
Seely, Helen B.
Seely, Charles A.
Seely, Ellen
Sayer, Walter H.
Sayer, Miss Jane S.
Sayer, Miss Mary G.
Showers, George
Shultz, Alice C.

Simms, John
Smith, Mrs. Susan R.
Smith, Joseph Hoyt
Stewart, Charles B.
Stewart, May
Seely Mrs. Mary Board
Thompson, Mrs. Mary F.
Thompson, Miss Camilla
Tuthill, John Bartlett
Tuthill, Hiram
Tuthill, Ledra
Tuthill, Charles S.
Thompson, Kittie E.
Van Kleeck, Miss C.
Vail, Mrs. Mary

Vail, Ada Bennett
Vail, Laura
Vollmer, Fred.
Vollmer, Mary
Vollmer, Edward C.
Vollmer, Albert
Walker, Jane C.
Wells, William A.
Wells, May A.
Wood, Mrs. Mary A.
Wood, Mrs. Helen A.
Wood, Mrs. Isabel K.
Wood, Helen King
Wanamaker, Willie D.

CHESTER CEMETERY.

The Home Altar.

Rev. R. H. McCready, Ph.D.

CHESTER is pre-eminently a home centre. Its homes are as permanent as any to be found in America. Its environment is rich in all that is conducive to make it a home centre. The fertility of its soil, the purity of its air, the beauty of its rolling and rugged landscape, the purity of its water, the great fields of the richest pasture, bordered and mingled with daisies and buttercups, makes it one of the most desirable places for a rural home to be found within twenty miles of the "American Rhine"—the grand Hudson River.

Its wheel roads and railroads are excellent, and it is not far distant from the great metropolis, New York City.

Nothing, however, is so important in any community as good homes. Almost anything else can be spared. But the home gives character to the community as it does to the individual. If the character of the home deteriorates, the whole community loses tone. Neither wealth, nor physical comforts, nor intellectual acumen, can make up for a home, lacking in affection or morality or spirituality.

It seems very fitting, therefore, that I should leave a few suggestions in this permanent form as to what seems to me to give the most exalted character and glory to the home. I refer to its religious foundation. "The Family Worship." Says the missionary John Paton:

"None of us can remember that any day ever passed unhallowed by family prayer. No hurry for market, no rush for business, no arrival of friends or guests, no trouble or sorrow, no joy or excitement ever prevented our kneeling around the family altar while the high priest (our father) led our prayers to God, and offered himself and his children there."

By family worship we mean "The adoration of God in the name of Christ" by the whole household, but conducted by its recognized head. The experience and history of the Church show that her spiritual vitality depends more on this institution than on any other outside of the pulpit. Her original constitution implies its use. And the strength, development and elevation of the soul for achievement in politics, commerce, letters, art, poetry, sculpture, architecture, painting, even in religion, on the part of the individuals in the nations and families where this God-given home institution has flourished, justifies us in claiming for it, in church and home, the recognition which God ordained.

The trail of divine glory which follows it where it is faithfully observed may be seen in every age grandly illuminating the darkness caused by superstition, ignorance and crime.

It is seen in the pathway of Noah and his family as they daily point the sinful world to God, the source of all their blessings, and sing the family song of praise within the ark, as it floats its family altar above a wrecked and ruined world.

Abraham the faithful is lifted into the loftiest of positions and his family preserved and distinguished more than any other in human history through the influence of family worship. He and his family are made the conservators of God's revelation; developed into the central nation in the history of the world; made the channel through which all the blessings of the redemption by Christ have flowed to mankind. What was the secret of it? God has revealed it in this declaration, "I know him that he will command his children and his household after him, and they shall keep the way of the Lord." To this day his devout descendants in all parts of the world, follow his example and keep up a family service. And when Moses, in Deut., 6th chapter, gives direction to the children of Israel for the realization of God's blessings, they include the family altar. He says: "These words which I command thee (by the Holy Spirit) this day shall be in thine heart, and thou shalt teach them diligently unto thy children . . . . . when thou liest down and when thou risest up." When Zechariah exhorts the people to repentance it is by families. Thus, throughout the Old Testament and continued as distinctly in the New, runs this golden thread of domestic religion. Cornelius and Apollos and Timothy learned to pray here, and on the model of this home altar of the Jew, the more spiritual family altar of the Christian has been based and continued for 1800 years with varied success. Neander says, "The early Christians began and closed the day with prayer." Jerome relates of the place where he lived that "at an early hour in the morning, the families were assembled, when a portion of scripture from the Old Testament was read which was followed by a hymn and a prayer. In the evening the family again assembled for the same service. When family worship was more general in Germany, Switzerland, Holland, France, Scotland, and England, the spiritual quickening was the greatest that the world has seen since the Christian era began. Its source is recognized by every fair writer as the family. Even the graceless but lofty bard of Scotland, Burns, has set in jeweled pictures the value and the living influence of this institution, in the "Cotter's Saturday Night."

> The cheerfu' supper done, wi' serious face,
> They round the ingle form a circle wide;
> The sire turns o'er wi' patriarchal grace
> The big *ha'* Bible ance his father's pride.
> He reads. They chant.
> Then kneeling down to heaven's eternal king,
> The saint, the father, and the husband prays.
> . . . .
> That thus they all shall meet in future days.
> Compared with this how poor religious pride
> . . . .
> When men display to congregations wide
> Devotions every grace except the heart.

True, there is no specific command for family worship in God's word. Neither is there a command to mothers to give nourishment to their children. Both these duties are implied. The child needs religion as it needs food daily. Many duties are implied rather than commanded. It is not a fossil, as many say, of the reformation period, too narrow, slow and cumbersome for this busy, liberal, progressive age. We ought to sustain it in the midst of our increased tension.

It was coeval with the first Church. It has lived through all changes. It was intended for these times of increased tension in the commercial, social and political life. It has given much of the spiritual life which the Presbyterian Church has enjoyed. The home altar is the glory of the Covenanter Church. It is the real life-giving source of every branch of the Church of Christ. It is the eternal light of the home. It shows to husband, wife, father, mother, child, sister, brother, the pathway to the New Jerusalem. God speaks to child and parent daily through it. It strengthens us daily against sin. It melts into tears and submission. It moves us to new resolutions. It inspires us to new sacrifices and new love. It arms each pilgrim with a stronger sword of the Word.

Let this be stamped by the Church on every life in her bounds. To this end I would suggest,

1. That the Church should teach distinctly and fully what the family is.

Modern industrialism, unintentionally it may be, is forcing new problems on the Christian home. The struggle for existence forces on the Christian father these questions, 'Can I compete with the man without wife and child in wages? If not, must my wife and child labor by my side for an existence? Since necessity says they must, and are thus made independent of me, what claim have they upon me, or I upon them?" Socialism answers, ' Convenience." "If we are living together only for convenience, would I not be justified in leaving them when work fails?" Yes, says the world; self first, self always.

Socialism, Mormonism, Materialism, Skepticism, each backed by its false philosophy of the family, is aided by free speech to destroy the Christian home. They each use both science and the Bible in proof of their theories. The Christian man needs help in the face of all these fallacies and temptations to defend his home. The Church should help him. It is my conviction that the Church should teach that the family is a divine institution, as is the Church and the State; that it is a moral organic entity.

It has a moral personality. Its will is not the will of the husband, or of the wife, but the will of both combined. The family once formed can not be dissolved from its organic relation. Adultery may be legal cause for separation, but that does not extinguish the family any more than the hanging of the murderer destroys the nation.

Were the family constituted simply by a compact, it could be broken or dissolved by mutual consent, like that of a bank, railroad, or stock exchange. This is the free-love theory, not the Christian. God constituted the family a moral organic entity in Adam and Eve. And Christ reiterated this doctrine when he said, "they are no more twain but one flesh."

The daily family worship is to guard and foster this organic life. But if men are ignorant of the fact that they are a part of such organic life, how shall they be able always to withstand the temptation put upon them by modern industrialism and false philosophy? Without knowing what the family is, to what shall the family aspire? If there is no family aspiration, what need of family worship? Blot out the family aspiration and the family worship, and the family organism, and you have individualism run mad.

The Church should call a halt on this radical individualism of our day by teaching the truth of God's word as to the moral organic life.

This leads to the statement,

II. That the Church should teach definitely the purpose of the family.

Little, evidently, is known of the purpose of the family by professed believers judging from the motive by which families are formed, or the manner in which they are conducted.

The Church should set forth distinctly that the purpose of the family is the realization of all that is good, and pure, and noble, and blessed on earth and in heaven. It is not alone to perpetuate the race, but to develop grace within the heart. The Church has sought to develop grace within the individual, but has neglected God's means. The family is one of the best of God's means to this end. But without the proper purpose before it, how can the family accomplish its destiny intelligently? Its purpose is to discipline the children that may come into it for the higher duties of Church and State.

It did this for Christ. To fulfil this purpose Mary is given a husband and a home. It is only in the seeking of this purpose that the highest conjugal love is realized, that the physical, mental, moral and spiritual development of the tender infant cast upon the parents' arms are attempted. The purpose should be definitely stated by the Church, and daily religion being as much a necessity for its realization as is bread, family worship in some form will be instituted and continued.

III. There should be a greater appreciation by the ministry of family worship as an assistant to it in gospel work. Two of the very richest gospel sermons of thirty minutes' each, with a prayer-meeting thrown in during each week of busy life, are not enough for a family. Yet many do not even get this much gospel food because they do not go to hear the gospel. Then when we consider that many of the sermons are erroneous, many scientific essays, some sadly etherial, some all bones and some with no bones, fat and flabby, we shall be impressed with the need of a family altar in every home. There the people will drink in the gospel pure and simple, and there the prayers will be orthodox. Dr. Alexander in his admirable treatise on "Family Worship" shows conclusively that the decline of piety in Germany, Switzerland, Scotland, and New England, was due more to the decay of family worship than to any other known cause.

Every successful reformation struggle of the Church—that of the Waldenses, of Huss, of Luther, of Wycliffe, of the Covenanters of Scotland —has aimed at the promotion of family worship. Without it there is no permanent reformation. The Puritans looked upon it as the handmaid of the pulpit and fought with Queen Elizabeth to maintain it. The reasons behind this struggle for it in history are solid as the sun behind the ray of light. The father needs the exercise of the Priest daily. The child needs the catechetical instruction. The home needs the divine influence. The sermon is better received and more useful where the family altar reigns. Were the catechism and Scripture taught now as one hundred years ago with all our additional aids, we would have a Church with more back bone, and a deeper piety. Let the family altar be a fixed institution of every Christian home, and the life of all within seeking harmony with the morning and evening prayer, and we will have less trouble with the midnight dance, with Sabbath desecration, gambling, theatre-going and the saloon in all its phases. Let the Minister look upon each family where worship is kept up daily, as a mission station fully equipped with Priest, Bible, altar. Let him feel that every chapter of the Bible read in the home helps him to a more intelligent and cultured field; that every question of the catechism or verse of Scripture recited, every prayer uttered in the house helps the Minister in preaching the gospel. Think of the power of 500 or 5,000 people bowed each day before the Throne asking help for the Minister; success for the Word; the stronger out-going of the Spirit. It is worth more than millions in the conversion of the heathen, in the elevation of society, in the preservation of home and country, in the building of of the Church. The people work better when they pray at home. The Minister preaches better. Every relationship and experience of life is more sanctified when the family altar burns bright with love and truth and peace, laid upon it daily by God in answer to prayer. When the Ministry appreciates the power of family worship fully as an aid to the pulpit, it will be promoted. They will see to it that an altar is erected in every home.

IV. The higher Church court might call attention from time to time to the fact that family worship is still obligatory in each home.

The Confession of Faith says: "God is to be worshipped everywhere in spirit and in truth; as in private families daily." All Presbyterians accept that, and it is obligatory until erased.

A directory also for conducting family worship, of probably 2,500 words, is found in the same book. The Covenanter Testimony condemns as error that it is unnecessary (for families) to worship God each day.

It is not claimed that the Confession of Faith is perfect, or that it is binding in the same sense as the divine Word. Its teaching may be accepted as a guide to the individual worshipper. The session or minister should require this divine obligation of every home that comes into the flock. The public record would be an incentive to the establishment of family altars—intensive little mission stations. Every minister is looked upon as a success who establishes a great number of mission stations. And the minister should be looked upon as a failure, who neither established or reported family altars in his parish. As much so at least as when he fails to add members to his congregation and build up the Church.

V. The people should be convinced of the blessings accruing from family worship. A frequent presentation of them by the minister might assist a great deal.

It would not be difficult to show these. It glorifies God. It purifies and builds up the Church. It elevates the nation. It increases the power of the Word, and of the preacher, and of the Holy Spirit. But above all it crowns the home and every member of the household with a power, a grace, a knowledge, a holiness, a peace, not otherwise obtainable.

Children learn obedience by example rather than by precept. How shall the parent teach his child obedience without recognizing God's will—God's government at the family altar? The boy is the father of the man and having learned religion from his father in his infancy it is this religion, largely, that he wears in manhood. What shall it be? At present where there is no family worship, often in the most politely religious homes, this is the order of the Sabbath day:

Bathe and change the dress more carefully than on any other day of the week, breakfast later than usual go to Church, listen or dream a sermon through, get through with the public service some way, and home to a better dinner than on other days. The rest of the day devoted to relaxation or business. Anything else would be Puritan you know. The religious part of the family life lost during the whole week.

John Stuart Mills' religion without faith was almost as good as this. It at least had discipline and obedience, but obedience without faith or love. This is not Christianity. Daily prayer at the home gives the child a devotional tendency. It learns here the method of prayer. It learns to fear sin, to seek holiness, because this is the thing that its Christian parent is daily asking. It learns to prize the love of the parent, since the parent breathes out his love in asking the best things of God for his child.

The Word read will give life as quickly at the home as at the public altar. It will at least be stamped in the heart of the child from infancy. It can never forget it. No wickedness can blot it out. Who knows that it may not be quickened into life in the murderer's cell?

Augustine could not escape, in study or pleasure, the voice of his mother's prayer at the family altar. Samuel and Timothy never wanted to forget their mother's prayer. And when all else fails, often the love of the parent expressed in prayer constrains the child to seek God, to reform his life, to love his home.

The daily family worship affords frequent opportunity for regeneration, conversion, for the increase of the Holy Spirit, for godly service, for discipline of mind and heart, for the inculcation of good habits. Even the servant and the stranger, as they often have, may learn of God here. It will preserve the conjugal affection between husband and wife. It will increase it. For when wisdom, love and health—all blessedness—are asked for the wife and mother, and guidance for the husband and father, that he may lead her and all their children to the blessed home above, it is a loftier story of love, perhaps, than he ever told his companion before their approach to the marriage altar. All wrongs are pardoned and the sun goes down on no wrath, as he asks that God forgive him as he forgives those who trespass against him.

And a balm is sought and found for all the wounds he may have caused in the home. Alienations and strifes in our domestic life cannot be wholly avoided, but no family can bow long around a holy family altar without harmony.

It is hard to pray aloud for those whom we have once loved, with hatred raging in the heart. And then the absent one is always remembered. The prayer maintains the fire of affection for him in the heart of the household, while God blesses him.

In sickness, how comforting to the Christian to have the household gathered around the invalid, to call out the sympathy of the Infinite Christ who was touched with our infirmities, wounded for our healing, to ask the great Physician to heal our diseases. In death, how sublime to hear a family say, "Thy will be done," "We shall meet again."

In success and reverse this family worship gives the balance to the domestic life.

"It consecrates every natural relation, and exalts human affections by expanding them into eternity."

"The night is far spent, the day is at hand: let us therefore cast off the works of darkness and let us put on the armor of light."

"Beloved duty may be hard: but when life ends
And all the hard things are gone by,
And every ache has been relieved
And every tear is wiped away
And softly on the ravished eye
Breaks the clear dawn of Heaven's day
Joy shall for grief make such amends
That we shall wonder that we grieved."

The Lord bless thee, and keep thee!
　The Lord make his face shine upon thee,
And be gracious unto thee:
　The Lord lift up his countenance upon thee.
And give thee peace. AMEN.

www.ingramcontent.com/pod-product-compliance
Lightning Source LLC
Chambersburg PA
CBHW030406170426
43202CB00010B/1517